Navigating the Foreign Policy Landscape: A Diplomat's Guide to the Five "Tan" ex-Soviet Republics

ROBERTO MIGUEL RODRIGUEZ

Copyright Page

TITLE: Navigating the Foreign Policy Landscape: A Diplomat's Guide to the Five "Tan" ex-Soviet Republics

1ST Edition

Table of Contents

Navigating the Foreign Policy Landscape: A Diplomat's Guide to the Five "Tan" ex-Soviet Republics

By Roberto Miguel Rodriguez

Chapter 1: Understanding the Foreign Policy Landscape

Introduction to the Five "Tan" Ex-Soviet Republics

Welcome to the "Introduction to the Five 'Tan' Ex-Soviet Republics subchapter." In this section, we will provide a comprehensive overview of the foreign policies of Kazakhstan, Kyrgyzstan, Tajikistan, Turkmenistan, and Uzbekistan. As diplomats, it is crucial to understand the intricacies and nuances of these nations to navigate the foreign policy landscape effectively.

The five "Tan" ex-Soviet republics emerged as independent states following the dissolution of the Soviet Union in 1991. Despite their shared Soviet past, each republic has developed unique foreign policy priorities, reflecting their history, geography, and socio-economic dynamics.

In this chapter, we will delve into various aspects of the foreign policies of these nations, highlighting key themes and challenges. We will explore their economic foreign policies, focusing on trade, investment, and development strategies. Additionally, we will examine their foreign energy policies, considering their rich natural resources and their role as major players in the global energy market.

Security is another crucial aspect of the foreign policies of these republics. We will analyze the regional security dynamics and the efforts made by these nations to combat terrorism, transnational crime, and border conflicts. Furthermore, we will explore their regional foreign policies, including their engagement with neighboring countries and regional organizations.

Culture and education play a significant role in shaping a nation's foreign policy. We will examine how the five "Tan" ex-Soviet republics utilize their cultural and educational diplomacy to promote their national interests and enhance their international influence.

The subchapter will also discuss these nations' trade and investment policies, highlighting their efforts to attract foreign direct investment and foster economic partnerships. We will explore their international alliances and partnerships, including their engagements with major powers and regional organizations.

Additionally, we will address the border and territorial disputes that have impacted the foreign policies of the five "Tan" ex-Soviet republics. Lastly, we will examine their diplomatic relations with major powers and their commitment to human rights and democracy promotion.

Through a comprehensive understanding of the foreign policies of these nations, diplomats can effectively engage with the five "Tan" ex-Soviet republics, fostering cooperation, resolving conflicts, and promoting mutual understanding. This subchapter will serve as a valuable guide for diplomats navigating the dynamic foreign policy landscape of Kazakhstan, Kyrgyzstan, Tajikistan, Turkmenistan, and Uzbekistan.

Overview of Diplomatic Relations with the Five "Tan" Ex-Soviet Republics

As diplomats, understanding the nuances of diplomatic relations with the five "Tan" ex-Soviet republics is crucial for navigating the dynamic foreign policy landscape. Kazakhstan, Kyrgyzstan, Tajikistan, Turkmenistan, and Uzbekistan each have unique diplomatic priorities, which we must comprehend to engage with these nations effectively. This subchapter provides a comprehensive overview of the diplomatic relations with these republics, shedding light on their economic, energy, security, regional, cultural, educational, trade, investment, international alliances, border and territorial disputes, as well as their relations with major powers and human rights and democracy promotion.

Economically, the five "Tan" ex-Soviet republics have adopted different approaches. Kazakhstan's diversified economy and vast energy resources make it an attractive investment destination, while Kyrgyzstan and Tajikistan focus on agriculture and rely on remittances from migrant workers. Turkmenistan's economy heavily depends on gas exports, whereas Uzbekistan has implemented market-oriented reforms to attract foreign investment and diversify its economy.

Energy foreign policy is a pivotal aspect of these republics' diplomatic strategies. Kazakhstan and Turkmenistan possess significant energy resources, making energy cooperation and export routes essential for economic growth. This chapter delves into the Caspian Sea's legal framework, pipeline politics, and regional energy projects, shedding light on their foreign energy policy complexities.

Security foreign policy is another critical area of focus. The five "Tan" ex-Soviet republics face common security challenges like terrorism, drug trafficking, and radicalization. Cooperation in counterterrorism, border management, and regional security organizations ensures regional stability.

This subchapter also explores the regional foreign policy of these republics. Central Asia's geopolitical dynamics, including relations with Russia, China, and other neighboring countries, shape their regional foreign policy. Understanding these dynamics is crucial for diplomats to identify areas of cooperation and potential conflicts.

Cultural and educational foreign policy plays a significant role in enhancing diplomatic relations. These republics actively promote cultural exchanges, scholarships, and academic partnerships to foster mutual understanding and strengthen people-to-people ties.

Trade and investment foreign policy focuses on attracting foreign direct investment, expanding trade relations, and fostering economic cooperation. This subchapter provides insights into each republic's investment climate, trade policies, and emerging sectors, enabling diplomats to identify potential areas for collaboration.

Furthermore, it explores the international alliances and partnerships of these republics, including their membership in organizations such as the Commonwealth of Independent States (CIS), Shanghai Cooperation Organization (SCO), and Eurasian Economic Union (EEU). Understanding the dynamics of these alliances is critical for diplomats to navigate the foreign policy landscape effectively.

Additionally, this subchapter examines border and territorial disputes, which have significant implications for regional stability. It sheds light on ongoing disputes and approaches to conflict resolution, providing diplomats with essential background information.

Lastly, human rights and democracy promotion are crucial components of foreign policy for these republics. Understanding their approach to human rights issues and democracy promotion is essential for diplomats to engage in constructive dialogue and advocate for positive change.

Overall, comprehending the diplomatic relations with the five "Tan" ex-Soviet republics is vital for diplomats navigating the foreign policy landscape. This subchapter provides an in-depth overview of their economic, energy, security, regional, cultural, educational, trade, investment, alliances, border disputes, relations with major powers, and human rights and democracy promotion. With this knowledge, diplomats can effectively engage with these nations, foster cooperation, and strengthen bilateral relations.

Analyzing the Key Players in the Foreign Policy Landscape

To navigate the complex foreign policy landscape of the five "Tan" ex-Soviet republics - Kazakhstan, Kyrgyzstan, Tajikistan, Turkmenistan, and Uzbekistan - diplomats must understand the key players shaping the region's diplomatic strategies. By examining the various aspects of foreign policy, including economic, energy, security, regional, cultural, educational, trade and investment, international alliances and partnerships, border and territorial disputes, diplomatic relations with major powers, and human rights and democracy promotion, diplomats can gain a comprehensive understanding of the dynamics at play in these countries.

Each of the five "Tan" ex-Soviet republics has unique key players who influence and shape their foreign policies. Understanding these individuals and institutions is crucial for diplomats seeking effective regional diplomacy.

Economically, the key players in these countries include government officials, business leaders, and foreign investors. Diplomats must know their goals, interests, and priorities to foster mutually beneficial economic relations.

In terms of energy, the key players are often state-owned companies, government agencies, and international energy corporations. Diplomats must understand the complex web of energy interests and the role of energy resources in shaping foreign policies.

Military leaders, intelligence agencies, and regional security organizations influence security foreign policy. Diplomats must navigate these relationships and understand the region's geopolitical challenges to ensure stability and cooperation.

Regional foreign policy is shaped by regional organizations, such as the Eurasian Economic Union and the Shanghai Cooperation Organization, as well as neighboring countries. Diplomats must engage with these organizations and build relationships with their counterparts in neighboring states to promote regional cooperation and address shared challenges.

Cultural and educational foreign policy involves key players such as cultural institutions, educational organizations, and diaspora communities. Diplomats must recognize the importance of cultural exchanges and educational partnerships in fostering mutual understanding and cooperation.

Government bodies, trade organizations, and foreign investors influence trade and investment foreign policy. Diplomats must facilitate trade agreements, promote investment opportunities, and address trade barriers.

International alliances and partnerships involve key players such as foreign ministries, international organizations, and non-governmental organizations. Diplomats must engage in multilateral diplomacy, foster alliances, and build partnerships to address global challenges and promote shared values.

Border and territorial disputes involve government officials, border control agencies, and international mediators. Diplomats must navigate these sensitive issues, promote peaceful resolutions, and work towards border stability.

Key players such as heads of state, foreign ministers, and diplomats shape diplomatic relations with major powers. Diplomats must build relationships with these individuals and engage in high-level diplomacy to promote the interests of their respective countries.

Lastly, human rights and democracy promotion involve civil society organizations, human rights activists, and international human rights bodies. Diplomats must advocate for human rights, support democratic institutions, and address human rights concerns in their engagement with these countries.

By analyzing the key players in the foreign policy landscape of the five "Tan" ex-Soviet republics, diplomats can better understand these countries' motivations, interests, and priorities. This knowledge will enable them to engage in effective diplomacy, foster cooperation, and navigate the complexities of the region's foreign policies.

Chapter 2: Economic Foreign Policy

Economic Overview of Kazakhstan

Kazakhstan, one of the five "Tan" ex-Soviet republics, has emerged as a dynamic and rapidly growing economy in Central Asia. With its vast natural resource reserves, strategic location, and proactive economic policies, Kazakhstan has positioned itself as a key player in the global marketplace. This section will overview Kazakhstan's economic landscape, highlighting its key sectors, trade relationships, and investment opportunities.

Kazakhstan's economy is primarily driven by its rich oil, natural gas, and mineral deposits. The country is among the world's top oil producers, and its energy sector has attracted significant foreign investment. Kazakhstan has substantially diversified its economy, focusing on sectors such as agriculture, manufacturing, and services. The government aims to reduce the country's dependence on oil and gas exports and foster sustainable economic growth.

In terms of trade, Kazakhstan has actively pursued regional and international partnerships. The country is a Eurasian Economic Union (EAEU) member and has signed numerous free trade agreements with neighboring countries and key global players. This has facilitated greater market access for Kazakhstani goods and services, boosting trade volumes and attracting foreign direct investment.

Favorable policies, attractive tax incentives, and a commitment to economic liberalization characterize Kazakhstan's investment climate. The government has implemented reforms to improve the ease of business, protect investor rights, and enhance transparency. Foreign investors are particularly drawn to the energy, mining, infrastructure, and agriculture sectors. Additionally, Kazakhstan's strategic location along the New Silk Road initiative positions it as a key transport and logistics hub, further enhancing its investment potential.

In conclusion, Kazakhstan's economic landscape presents significant opportunities for foreign diplomats and investors. The country's diversified economy, strategic location, and proactive policies make it an attractive destination for trade and investment. By understanding Kazakhstan's economic strengths and priorities, diplomats can effectively engage with the country in areas such as trade promotion, investment facilitation, and economic cooperation.

Economic Overview of Kyrgyzstan

Kyrgyzstan, one of the five "Tan" ex-Soviet republics, is a landlocked country in Central Asia. With a population of approximately 6.5 million, the country has a mixed economy heavily dependent on agriculture, mining, and services.

In recent years, Kyrgyzstan has made significant progress in economic reforms and attracting foreign investment. The government has implemented policies to promote a business-friendly environment, including reducing bureaucracy and corruption and improving the legal framework for investment.

The country's main industries include mining, particularly gold and uranium extraction, agriculture, textiles, and tourism. Kyrgyzstan is known for its abundant mineral resources, which have attracted foreign investors and contributed to economic growth. The agricultural sector plays a vital role in the country's economy, with the production of wheat, potatoes, cotton, and dairy products major contributors to the GDP.

However, despite these positive developments, Kyrgyzstan faces various challenges in its economic landscape. The country continues to struggle with poverty, unemployment, and income inequality. Limited access to credit and lack of infrastructure pose significant barriers to economic growth and development.

Furthermore, Kyrgyzstan's economy is vulnerable to external shocks, such as fluctuations in commodity prices and regional conflicts. The country's heavy dependence on remittances from migrant workers, especially those in Russia and Kazakhstan, also exposes its economy to external risks.

The Kyrgyz government has been actively pursuing economic diversification and regional integration to address these challenges. It has sought to strengthen trade ties with neighboring countries and participate in regional economic initiatives such as the Eurasian Economic Union and the Belt and Road Initiative.

Foreign diplomats engaging with Kyrgyzstan should consider the country's economic landscape when formulating their foreign policy strategies. Supporting initiatives promoting economic diversification, attracting foreign investment, and improving infrastructure can contribute to Kyrgyzstan's economic development and stability.

Overall, Kyrgyzstan presents both opportunities and challenges in its economic landscape. By understanding the country's economic dynamics and working towards sustainable and inclusive growth, diplomats can play a crucial role in fostering economic cooperation and enhancing bilateral relations between Kyrgyzstan and their respective countries.

Economic Overview of Tajikistan

Tajikistan, one of the five "Tan" ex-Soviet republics, is a landlocked country in Central Asia. With a population of over 9 million people, Tajikistan faces numerous economic challenges as it strives to develop its economy and improve its citizens' living standards. As diplomats engaged in shaping foreign policy, understanding the economic landscape of Tajikistan is crucial in effectively engaging with the country.

Tajikistan's economy heavily relies on agriculture, accounting for about one-third of the country's GDP. The main agricultural products include cotton, fruits, vegetables, and livestock. However, the agricultural sector faces significant challenges due to limited access to modern farming techniques, lack of infrastructure, and vulnerability to climate change.

In recent years, Tajikistan has tried diversifying its economy and reducing its agricultural dependence. The country has significant mining potential, with gold, silver, and uranium deposits. Additionally, Tajikistan has been exploring its hydropower potential by constructing several hydroelectric power plants. These initiatives aim to boost economic growth and provide a reliable energy source for domestic consumption and export.

Despite these efforts, Tajikistan faces various obstacles to economic development. The country struggles with high unemployment rates, especially among the youth, and widespread poverty. Limited access to education and healthcare services further hinders economic progress.

The government of Tajikistan has implemented economic reforms to attract foreign investment and stimulate economic growth. It has introduced measures to improve the business climate, simplify regulations, and reduce corruption. However, significant challenges remain, including a weak legal framework, inadequate infrastructure, and limited access to finance.

Regarding international trade, Tajikistan has sought to diversify its export markets. The country primarily exports aluminium, cotton, and textiles. Russia, China, and Turkey are among its major trading partners. Tajikistan is also a member of the World Trade Organization, facilitating its integration into the global economy.

As diplomats, understanding the economic challenges and opportunities in Tajikistan is crucial for engaging with the country effectively. By supporting initiatives that promote economic diversification, improve infrastructure, and enhance the business climate, diplomats can contribute to Tajikistan's economic development and foster stronger bilateral relations.

Economic Overview of Turkmenistan

As one of the five "Tan" ex-Soviet republics, Turkmenistan has made significant strides in its economic development since gaining independence in 1991. With a diverse range of natural resources, including natural gas, oil, and cotton, the country has the potential to become an economic powerhouse in Central Asia.

Turkmenistan's economy relies heavily on its energy sector, particularly natural gas exports. The country possesses the world's fourth-largest natural gas reserves, allowing it to establish itself as a key player in the global energy market. This has also enabled Turkmenistan to forge strong economic ties with major powers, including China, Russia, and Iran, who are key consumers of its natural gas.

However, the overreliance on the energy sector has challenged Turkmenistan's economic diversification. The government has recognized the need to reduce its dependency on natural gas exports and promote the agriculture, manufacturing, and tourism sectors. Efforts have been made to attract foreign direct investment and create a more business-friendly environment, but progress has been slow.

Turkmenistan's economic policies are characterized by a centralized state-led approach, with the government playing a dominant role in the economy. The country has implemented a series of economic reforms to modernise and liberalise its economy. These reforms include the introduction of a market-based exchange rate system, the establishment of special economic zones, and the simplification of business registration processes.

Another important aspect of Turkmenistan's economic policy is its focus on infrastructure development. The government has invested heavily in infrastructure projects, such as the construction of highways, railways, and airports, to improve connectivity within the country and enhance its trade potential.

Despite these efforts, Turkmenistan still faces several economic challenges. A lack of transparency, corruption, and limited access to credit characterizes the country's business environment. The government's economic control has also hindered private sector growth and innovation.

In conclusion, Turkmenistan's economic development has been largely driven by its energy sector, particularly natural gas exports. The government recognizes the need to diversify its economy and attract foreign investment to promote agriculture, manufacturing, and tourism sectors. Infrastructure development is also a key focus for the country. However, challenges such as a centralized economy, lack of transparency, and corruption continue to hinder Turkmenistan's economic potential.

Economic Overview of Uzbekistan

Uzbekistan, one of the five "Tan" ex-Soviet republics, has undergone significant economic transformations since gaining independence in 1991. As diplomats navigating the foreign policy landscape of the region, it is crucial to understand the economic dynamics of Uzbekistan to engage with its government and people effectively.

Uzbekistan boasts a diversified economy, with sectors such as agriculture, mining, manufacturing, and services contributing to its growth. The agricultural sector, in particular, plays a vital role in the country's economy, employing a significant portion of the population and contributing to its self-sufficiency in food production.

Over the years, Uzbekistan has implemented various economic reforms to attract foreign investment and promote economic growth. The government has focused on improving the business environment, simplifying bureaucratic procedures, and implementing market-oriented policies. These efforts have steadily increased foreign direct investment, particularly in sectors such as energy, infrastructure, and telecommunications.

The energy sector is a crucial component of Uzbekistan's economy, with the country being rich in natural resources. It has significant oil, natural gas, and minerals reserves, making it an attractive destination for energy investment. The government has been actively working to diversify its energy exports and strengthen its position as a regional energy hub.

Uzbekistan has also prioritized regional cooperation and integration to boost its economic growth. It is a member of various regional organizations, such as the Eurasian Economic Union and the Shanghai Cooperation Organization, which provide opportunities for trade and investment. The country has actively pursued regional infrastructure projects, including constructing transportation corridors and developing free economic zones.

Despite its economic progress, Uzbekistan faces challenges like corruption, inadequate infrastructure, and a skilled labor shortage. As diplomats, understanding these challenges and advocating for reforms can contribute to the country's economic development.

In conclusion, Uzbekistan's economy has experienced significant transformations since gaining independence. The government's focus on economic reforms, regional cooperation, and attracting foreign investment has contributed to its growth and diversification. As diplomats engaging with Uzbekistan, it is crucial to recognize the country's economic potential and work towards addressing its challenges to promote sustainable economic development and strengthen bilateral relations.

Chapter 3: Energy Foreign Policy

Energy Resources and Strategy in Kazakhstan

Kazakhstan, one of the five "Tan" ex-Soviet republics, possesses vast energy resources that have played a crucial role in shaping its foreign policy. As diplomats navigating the foreign policy landscape of Kazakhstan, it is important to understand the country's energy resources and the strategies it employs to leverage them in the international arena.

Kazakhstan has abundant reserves of oil, natural gas, and uranium. Its oil reserves are estimated to be the eleventh largest in the world, while it holds the second-largest natural gas reserves among former Soviet republics. Additionally, Kazakhstan is the world's leading uranium producer. These resources have positioned Kazakhstan as a significant player in the global energy market and have shaped its foreign policy priorities.

Energy security is a top concern for Kazakhstan, as it seeks to diversify its energy exports and reduce its reliance on a single market. This strategy has driven Kazakhstan to forge partnerships with multiple countries and develop extensive pipeline infrastructure. The country has established the Caspian Pipeline Consortium, which transports oil from the Caspian Sea to the Russian Black Sea port of Novorossiysk. It has also collaborated with China on constructing the Kazakhstan-China Pipeline, facilitating energy exports to the growing Asian market.

Furthermore, Kazakhstan actively seeks foreign investment in its energy sector to enhance its production capabilities and attract advanced technologies. It has attracted major international oil companies through favorable investment conditions and partnerships with state-owned enterprises. This approach has boosted Kazakhstan's energy sector and strengthened its diplomatic ties with countries investing in its resources.

Regarding international alliances, Kazakhstan is a founding member of the Eurasian Economic Union (EAEU) and the Shanghai Cooperation Organization (SCO). These alliances provide Kazakhstan a platform to promote its energy interests and establish closer economic and political ties with neighboring countries.

However, the development of energy resources in Kazakhstan is not without challenges. Environmental concerns, infrastructure limitations, and geopolitical complexities pose significant hurdles to the country's energy strategy. Diplomats must be aware of these challenges and work towards finding sustainable solutions that balance economic growth with environmental considerations and regional dynamics.

In conclusion, energy resources are pivotal in shaping Kazakhstan's foreign policy. The country's vast oil, natural gas, and uranium reserves drive its energy security agenda, prompting it to diversify its energy exports and seek foreign investment. As diplomats, understanding Kazakhstan's energy resources and strategies is crucial to navigating its foreign policy landscape and fostering fruitful partnerships in the energy sector.

Energy Resources and Strategy in Kyrgyzstan

Kyrgyzstan, one of the five "Tan" ex-Soviet republics, possesses diverse energy resources. The country has significant hydropower potential with its mountainous terrain, making it an important player in the regional energy landscape. This subchapter delves into Kyrgyzstan's energy resources and strategies, shedding light on its foreign policy implications.

Hydropower is the primary energy resource in Kyrgyzstan, accounting for nearly 95% of its electricity production. The country boasts numerous rivers and lakes, making it an ideal location for hydropower development. Kyrgyzstan's abundant water resources offer a renewable and sustainable energy solution for both domestic consumption and regional energy exports.

Given its strategic location in Central Asia, Kyrgyzstan's energy resources have become crucial to its foreign policy. The country has actively pursued energy cooperation with its neighbors, particularly Kazakhstan and Tajikistan, through regional initiatives such as the Central Asia Regional Economic Cooperation (CAREC) program. These collaborations enhance energy security, promote economic integration, and foster regional stability.

Kyrgyzstan's energy strategy also involves diversifying its energy mix to reduce reliance on hydropower. The country has explored the potential for renewable energy sources such as solar and wind. This approach aligns with global efforts to combat climate change while ensuring energy security.

However, Kyrgyzstan faces challenges in fully harnessing its energy potential. The country's ageing infrastructure and limited technical expertise hinder its energy resource development and efficient utilization. Additionally, Kyrgyzstan's energy sector is susceptible to seasonal variations and climate change, affecting the reliability of its energy supply.

Kyrgyzstan seeks to attract foreign investment and technological expertise to address these challenges. The country aims to forge partnerships with international players in the energy sector through its foreign policy initiatives. Collaborations with countries like China, Russia, and Turkey have emerged as key investment and technological transfer avenues.

In conclusion, Kyrgyzstan's energy resources, particularly hydropower, play a vital role in its foreign policy. The country's pursuit of energy cooperation, diversification, and attracting foreign investment are crucial strategies to enhance energy security, promote economic development, and foster regional stability. By leveraging its energy potential and forging strategic partnerships, Kyrgyzstan aims to position itself as a significant player in the regional energy landscape.

Energy Resources and Strategy in Tajikistan

Tajikistan, one of the five "Tan" ex-Soviet republics, possesses significant energy resources crucial in shaping its foreign policy. This subchapter explores Tajikistan's energy resources and strategies, shedding light on their impact on the country's diplomatic relations and economic foreign policy.

Tajikistan is blessed with abundant renewable energy resources, particularly hydropower. The country boasts numerous rivers and mountainous terrain, making it well-suited for hydroelectric power generation. With an estimated potential to generate around 527 billion kWh of electricity annually, Tajikistan can meet its domestic energy needs and export surplus electricity to neighboring countries.

The availability of such energy resources has allowed Tajikistan to develop a strategic approach in its foreign policy. By positioning itself as a regional energy hub, Tajikistan aims to enhance its influence and strengthen diplomatic ties with its neighbors. It has actively engaged in energy cooperation agreements with countries like Afghanistan, Uzbekistan, and Kyrgyzstan, fostering regional energy integration and promoting stability.

Moreover, Tajikistan's energy resources have helped shape its economic foreign policy. The country has sought to leverage its hydroelectric potential to attract foreign direct investment (FDI) in the energy sector. By offering favorable conditions, such as tax incentives and simplified regulations, Tajikistan aims to encourage international companies to invest in its energy infrastructure, contributing to economic growth and job creation.

However, challenges exist in fully harnessing Tajikistan's energy potential. Limited financial resources and technological capabilities hinder the country from exploiting its energy resources to their fullest extent. As a result, Tajikistan has sought international partnerships and alliances to overcome these obstacles. Collaborations with countries like China Russia and international organizations such as the World Bank and Asian Development Bank have supported Tajikistan's energy sector development.

Furthermore, Tajikistan's energy resources and strategy have implications for its security foreign policy. The dependence of neighboring countries on Tajikistan's electricity exports creates interdependencies, which can contribute to regional stability. By providing reliable energy supplies, Tajikistan can enhance its security cooperation with neighboring states, promoting regional peace and stability.

In conclusion, Tajikistan's energy resources and strategy significantly affect its foreign policy. The country's abundant hydroelectric potential allows it to pursue a regional energy hub status, attract foreign investment, and strengthen diplomatic relations. However, challenges remain, necessitating international partnerships fully exploiting its energy resources. By effectively managing its energy sector, Tajikistan can meet its domestic energy needs, shape its foreign policy objectives, and contribute to regional stability.

Energy Resources and Strategy in Turkmenistan

As diplomats navigate the foreign policy landscape of the five "Tan" ex-Soviet republics, understanding each country's energy resources and strategies is crucial. In Turkmenistan, a nation known for its abundant natural gas reserves, energy plays a central role in its domestic and foreign policy.

Turkmenistan boasts the world's fourth-largest natural gas reserves, making it a key player in the global energy market. With increasing demand for cleaner and more sustainable energy sources, Turkmenistan's vast reserves position the country as a potential supplier to international markets. This has shaped the country's energy foreign policy, as Turkmenistan seeks to diversify its energy exports and establish strategic partnerships with key stakeholders.

One of Turkmenistan's major energy strategies is the construction of pipelines to transport its natural gas to global markets. The Turkmenistan-Afghanistan-Pakistan-India (TAPI) pipeline is a significant project that aims to connect Turkmenistan's gas fields with energy-hungry markets in South Asia. Turkmenistan aims to bolster economic ties and promote regional stability by enhancing regional energy cooperation and infrastructure development.

Additionally, Turkmenistan has pursued partnerships with major powers to maximize the potential of its energy resources. The country has engaged in diplomatic relations with Russia, China, and the European Union, among others, to attract foreign investment and technological expertise. These alliances support Turkmenistan's energy sector and contribute to its broader economic development and geopolitical influence.

However, Turkmenistan's energy resources and strategy are not without challenges. The country heavily relies on natural gas exports, making it vulnerable to fluctuations in global energy prices.

Diversifying its energy portfolio and exploring alternative energy sources are essential to ensure long-term sustainability and resilience.

Moreover, Turkmenistan's energy foreign policy must navigate complex regional dynamics and border disputes. The country faces territorial disputes with neighboring countries, such as Uzbekistan, over shared energy resources and transportation routes. Balancing energy interests with diplomatic relations and maintaining regional stability is delicate for Turkmenistan's diplomats.

In conclusion, Turkmenistan's energy resources and strategy play a significant role in shaping the country's foreign policy. With vast natural gas reserves and ambitious pipeline projects, Turkmenistan seeks to maximize the potential of its energy sector and establish strategic partnerships with key stakeholders. However, global energy market fluctuations and regional disputes pose obstacles that diplomats must navigate. By understanding Turkmenistan's energy resources and strategies, diplomats can effectively engage with the country and contribute to regional stability and economic development.

Energy Resources and Strategy in Uzbekistan

Uzbekistan, one of the five "Tan" ex-Soviet republics, is endowed with abundant energy resources, making it a key player in the energy landscape of Central Asia. The country boasts significant natural gas, oil, and coal reserves strategically used to drive economic growth and shape its foreign policy.

As diplomats navigating the foreign policy landscape of Uzbekistan, it is crucial to understand the energy resources and strategy of the country. Uzbekistan's energy sector plays a vital role in shaping its economic foreign policy, as energy exports contribute significantly to its GDP and act as a catalyst for economic development.

The country's energy strategy focuses on diversification in terms of energy sources and export routes. Uzbekistan has been actively exploring alternative energy sources, such as renewable and nuclear power, to reduce its dependence on fossil fuels. This diversification strategy aligns with the global sustainable and clean energy solutions trend.

Regarding export routes, Uzbekistan has strategically expanded its energy infrastructure to ensure connectivity with neighboring countries and beyond. The construction of pipelines, such as the Turkmenistan-Uzbekistan-Kazakhstan-China gas pipeline, has enhanced its energy export capabilities and strengthened regional cooperation. Furthermore, Uzbekistan's participation in international alliances and partnerships, such as the Shanghai Cooperation Organization and the Eurasian Economic Union, has facilitated energy cooperation and trade with other countries.

However, Uzbekistan's energy resources and strategy also pose challenges and raise important considerations in security and border disputes. The geopolitical dynamics of Central Asia, coupled with territorial disputes, can impact the stability and reliability of energy supply in the region. Diplomatic efforts must be directed towards resolving these issues and fostering a secure environment for energy cooperation.

Moreover, as diplomats, it is essential to address the social and environmental impact of energy development. Uzbekistan's energy strategy must prioritize sustainable practices and protect human rights and democratic principles. This includes promoting transparency, accountability, and citizen participation in decision-making processes related to energy projects.

In conclusion, understanding Uzbekistan's energy resources and strategy is crucial for diplomats navigating the foreign policy landscape of the five "Tan" ex-Soviet republics. The country's energy sector shapes its economic foreign policy, regional cooperation, and international alliances. By addressing the challenges and opportunities presented by Uzbekistan's energy resources, diplomats can contribute to the sustainable development and stability of the region.

Chapter 4: Security Foreign Policy

Security Challenges in Kazakhstan

As one of the five "Tan" ex-Soviet republics, Kazakhstan faces a range of security challenges that require careful consideration and strategic planning. This subchapter aims to shed light on the key security challenges in Kazakhstan and provide insights for diplomats navigating the foreign policy landscape.

One of the primary security concerns in Kazakhstan is terrorism and extremism. The country's geographical location, sharing borders with volatile regions such as Afghanistan, makes it susceptible to the spillover effects of radical ideologies and insurgent activities. Diplomats must understand and address the root causes of extremism while strengthening cooperation with international partners to counter this threat effectively.

Another significant security challenge is the proliferation of illicit drugs and organized crime. Kazakhstan is a transit point for drug trafficking routes from Afghanistan to Europe and Russia, further exacerbating the security situation. Diplomats should prioritize enhancing regional and international cooperation to combat drug trafficking networks, strengthen border controls, and promote cross-border law enforcement initiatives.

Furthermore, Kazakhstan faces the challenge of cyber threats and information warfare. With the increasing reliance on digital systems and connectivity, the country is vulnerable to cyberattacks that can disrupt critical infrastructure, compromise national security, and undermine public trust. Diplomats must advocate for robust cybersecurity measures, foster international collaboration, and promote the exchange of best practices to address this evolving threat effectively.

Additionally, the issue of separatism and ethnic tensions poses security challenges in Kazakhstan. The country is home to various ethnic groups, and tensions occasionally arise, particularly in areas with a significant non-Kazakh population. Diplomats should support policies that promote inclusivity, dialogue, and cultural understanding to mitigate these tensions and foster social cohesion.

Lastly, Kazakhstan's nuclear non-proliferation efforts are crucial for regional and global security. As a former nuclear state and the Semipalatinsk nuclear test site host, Kazakhstan has played a vital role in nuclear disarmament initiatives. Diplomats should advocate for strengthening non-proliferation frameworks, support nuclear security measures, and encourage peaceful uses of nuclear energy.

In conclusion, Kazakhstan faces various security challenges that require a comprehensive and multidimensional approach. Diplomats must engage with their counterparts, international organizations, and regional partners to address terrorism, drug trafficking, cyber threats, ethnic tensions, and nuclear non-proliferation effectively. By understanding and addressing these challenges, diplomats can contribute to the stability and security of Kazakhstan and the entire region.

Security Challenges in Kyrgyzstan

As diplomats navigate the complex foreign policy landscape of the five "Tan" ex-Soviet republics, it is crucial to understand the security challenges faced by each country. In the case of Kyrgyzstan, this landlocked nation has unique security concerns that demand attention and strategic planning.

One of the primary security challenges in Kyrgyzstan is the threat of terrorism and extremism. The country shares borders with Afghanistan and Tajikistan, making it vulnerable to the spillover effects of regional conflicts and the activities of extremist groups. The porous borders and rugged terrain provide opportunities for illicit activities, including drug trafficking and arms smuggling. Diplomats must share intelligence and collaborate with international partners to counter these threats effectively.

Furthermore, Kyrgyzstan faces internal security challenges, including political instability and social unrest. The country has experienced multiple revolutions and ethnic tensions, leading to sporadic violence and civil unrest. Diplomats must work closely with the Kyrgyz government to promote stability, strengthen democratic institutions, and address the root causes of social and political discontent.

Another significant security concern in Kyrgyzstan is the management of its natural resources. The country is rich in minerals, including gold and uranium, which attract foreign investment and stimulate economic growth. However, exploiting these resources can lead to environmental degradation, corruption, and social inequality. Diplomats must advocate for sustainable resource management practices and promote transparency to prevent conflicts and ensure the equitable distribution of wealth.

In addition to these challenges, Kyrgyzstan faces cybersecurity threats and potential external interference in its domestic affairs. Diplomats must prioritize cooperation on cybersecurity, support local capacity building, and promote responsible behavior in cyberspace.

To address these security challenges effectively, diplomats should engage in multilateral and bilateral partnerships, including regional organizations such as the Collective Security Treaty Organization (CSTO) and the Shanghai Cooperation Organization (SCO). These alliances provide a platform for cooperation and coordination on security issues, enhancing Kyrgyzstan's capacity to respond to emerging threats.

In conclusion, Kyrgyzstan faces a range of security challenges that require diplomats' attention and strategic efforts. By addressing the threats of terrorism, political instability, resource management, cybersecurity, and external interference, diplomats can contribute to the stability and security of Kyrgyzstan, promoting peace and prosperity in the region.

Security Challenges in Tajikistan

Tajikistan, one of the five "Tan" ex-Soviet republics, faces various security challenges that have significant implications for its foreign policy. This subchapter explores the key security issues in Tajikistan and their impact on regional stability, focusing on the concerns of diplomats involved in the foreign policy landscape of the five "Tan" republics.

Tajikistan's security challenges are multifaceted and interconnected, stemming from internal and external factors. Internally, the country grapples with the threat of terrorism, extremism, and organized crime. The presence of various militant groups, including the Islamic Movement of Uzbekistan (IMU) and the Taliban, poses a significant risk to the stability of Tajikistan and the wider Central Asian region. These groups exploit porous borders and weak governance structures to conduct illicit activities, such as drug trafficking and arms smuggling.

Externally, Tajikistan's security is influenced by regional dynamics and geopolitical rivalries. The country shares a border with Afghanistan, a volatile state plagued by conflict and insurgency. Instability in Afghanistan directly impacts Tajikistan's security, as it can lead to an influx of refugees, cross-border violence, and the spillover of extremist ideologies. Moreover, Tajikistan is caught in geopolitical competition between major powers, such as Russia, China, and the United States, which can exacerbate security challenges.

A multifaceted approach has characterized Tajikistan's foreign policy response to these security challenges. Firstly, the country has strengthened its bilateral and multilateral security cooperation with regional and international partners. Tajikistan is an active member of the Collective Security Treaty Organization (CSTO) and maintains close ties with Russia, which provides military assistance and training. Additionally, Tajikistan participates in various regional initiatives, such as the Shanghai Cooperation Organization (SCO), to enhance security cooperation and coordination.

Secondly, Tajikistan has prioritized border security and counterterrorism efforts. The country has invested in strengthening its border infrastructure, enhancing border control capabilities, and conducting joint military exercises with neighboring countries. Tajikistan has also increased counterterrorism cooperation within the framework of the SCO and CSTO, sharing intelligence and conducting joint operations to combat extremist threats.

Lastly, Tajikistan recognizes the importance of addressing the root causes of security challenges. The country has implemented socioeconomic development programs focusing on poverty reduction, education, and job creation. By addressing the underlying grievances and socioeconomic disparities that fuel extremism, Tajikistan aims to promote stability and resilience.

In conclusion, Tajikistan faces significant security challenges, including terrorism, extremism, and geopolitical rivalries. These challenges impact Tajikistan's internal stability and have broader regional implications. Diplomats involved in the foreign policy landscape of the five "Tan" republics must understand and address these security challenges to promote stability and cooperation in the region.

Security Challenges in Turkmenistan

Turkmenistan, one of the five "Tan" ex-Soviet republics, faces various security challenges that require careful consideration and deliberation by diplomats. This subchapter aims to shed light on the security landscape of Turkmenistan, providing valuable insights for diplomats navigating the foreign policy terrain.

One of Turkmenistan's most pressing security challenges is the threat of transnational organized crime. At the crossroads of major drug trafficking routes, Turkmenistan faces the constant risk of drug smuggling, money laundering, and human trafficking. These criminal activities undermine the rule of law and pose a significant threat to regional stability. Diplomats must cooperate with their Turkmenistan counterparts to develop comprehensive strategies to combat transnational organized crime and strengthen law enforcement capabilities.

Another critical security challenge in Turkmenistan is terrorism and extremism. While the country has managed to maintain relative stability compared to its neighbors, the rise of extremist ideologies in the region poses a constant threat. Diplomats should work closely with Turkmen authorities to enhance intelligence sharing, capacity building, and counter-terrorism efforts. Regional cooperation and collaboration between Turkmenistan and its neighboring countries are crucial in addressing this shared security concern.

Turkmenistan's energy infrastructure also presents security challenges. As a significant exporter of natural gas, Turkmenistan's energy facilities and pipelines are potential targets for sabotage and disruption. Diplomats should prioritize cooperation with Turkmenistan in developing robust security measures to safeguard critical energy infrastructure, ensuring uninterrupted energy supply to regional and international markets.

Additionally, Turkmenistan faces challenges related to border security and territorial disputes. Disputes over borders and territories can lead to tensions and conflicts, threatening regional stability. Diplomats must actively engage in dialogue and negotiations to resolve these disputes peacefully, promoting confidence-building measures and adherence to international law.

In conclusion, Turkmenistan faces various security challenges, including transnational organized crime, terrorism and extremism, energy infrastructure security, and border disputes. Diplomats must actively address these challenges, promoting regional cooperation, intelligence sharing, and capacity building. By working closely with Turkmen authorities and neighboring countries, diplomats can enhance security and stability in Turkmenistan and the wider region.

Security Challenges in Uzbekistan

Uzbekistan, one of the five "Tan" ex-Soviet republics, faces a range of security challenges that have significant implications for its internal stability and foreign policy. These challenges arise from various sources, including regional conflicts, terrorism, and transnational organized crime. Understanding these security challenges is crucial for diplomats engaged in the foreign policy landscape of the region.

One of the primary security challenges in Uzbekistan is its proximity to Afghanistan, a country plagued by decades of conflict and instability. The porous border between the two nations has facilitated the flow of narcotics, arms, and militants across the region. Uzbekistan's government has been actively countering this threat by cooperating with international partners and strengthening its border security measures.

Terrorism remains a persistent security concern for Uzbekistan. The country has experienced several terrorist attacks, including the deadly bombings in Tashkent in 1999. Uzbek extremists have also been involved in international terrorist activities, such as joining ISIS in the Middle East. The Uzbek government has implemented counterterrorism measures, including cracking down on extremist groups and promoting deradicalization programs.

Transnational organized crime poses another significant security challenge for Uzbekistan. The country is a transit route for drug trafficking from Afghanistan to Europe and Russia. Additionally, it faces challenges related to human trafficking, money laundering, and cybercrime. Uzbekistan has been enhancing its law enforcement capabilities and improving regional cooperation to combat these transnational criminal activities.

Uzbekistan's security challenges have implications for its foreign policy. The government has prioritized regional cooperation to address common security concerns. It participates actively in regional security organizations such as the Shanghai Cooperation Organization (SCO) and the Collective Security Treaty Organization (CSTO). Uzbekistan's engagement in these alliances aims to enhance its security capabilities and foster stability in the region.

In conclusion, Uzbekistan confronts various security challenges, including its proximity to Afghanistan, terrorism, and transnational organized crime. These challenges have shaped Uzbekistan's foreign policy priorities, leading to increased regional cooperation and engagement in security alliances. Diplomats engaged in the foreign policy landscape of the "Tan" ex-Soviet republics must be aware of these security challenges and work towards promoting stability and security in Uzbekistan and the wider region.

Chapter 5: Regional Foreign Policy

Regional Dynamics in Kazakhstan

Kazakhstan, the largest and most prosperous of the five "Tan" ex-Soviet republics, plays a crucial role in shaping the regional dynamics in Central Asia. This subchapter will delve into the regional dynamics within Kazakhstan and its impact on the broader foreign policy landscape of the "Tan" republics.

Kazakhstan's regional foreign policy is characterized by its commitment to promoting stability, economic development, and cooperation among its neighbors. As a landlocked country, Kazakhstan recognizes the importance of regional integration in overcoming geographical constraints and fostering mutual prosperity. The country actively participates in regional organizations such as the Shanghai Cooperation Organization (SCO) and the Eurasian Economic Union (EEU), seeking to enhance economic ties and strengthen security cooperation with its neighbors.

Economically, Kazakhstan's foreign policy prioritizes regional trade and investment. The country's vast energy resources, including oil and natural gas, make it a key player in the Central Asian energy market. Kazakhstan actively seeks to diversify its energy export routes, collaborating with neighboring countries to develop pipeline infrastructure and ensure regional energy security. Kazakhstan promotes cross-border trade, infrastructure development, and regional connectivity through initiatives like the Central Asia Regional Economic Cooperation program.

Security is another crucial aspect of Kazakhstan's regional foreign policy. The country is committed to combatting transnational threats such as terrorism, drug trafficking, and organized crime, recognizing the importance of regional cooperation in addressing these challenges effectively. Kazakhstan actively engages in security dialogues and joint military exercises with its regional partners to enhance collective security and stability.

Kazakhstan also significantly emphasises cultural and educational exchanges in its regional foreign policy. The country promotes people-to-people contacts, student exchanges, and cultural events to foster mutual understanding and strengthen regional ties. Kazakhstan's capital city, Nur-Sultan, hosts the Congress of Leaders of World and Traditional Religions, emphasizing its commitment to interfaith dialogue and cooperation.

In conclusion, Kazakhstan's regional dynamics play a vital role in shaping the foreign policy landscape of the "Tan" ex-Soviet republics. Kazakhstan strives to foster stability, prosperity, and mutual understanding within the region through its focus on economic cooperation, security collaboration, cultural exchanges, and regional integration. As diplomats navigating the foreign policy landscape of the "Tan" republics, understanding and engaging with the regional dynamics in Kazakhstan is crucial for promoting peace, development, and cooperation in Central Asia.

Regional Dynamics in Kyrgyzstan

Kyrgyzstan, one of the five "Tan" ex-Soviet republics, is a landlocked country in Central Asia. This subchapter will delve into the regional dynamics that shape its foreign policy and diplomatic relations with other countries.

Kyrgyzstan's regional dynamics are influenced by its geographical location and historical ties. Situated in the heart of Central Asia, it shares borders with Kazakhstan, Tajikistan, Uzbekistan, and China.

These neighboring countries are vital in shaping Kyrgyzstan's foreign policy decisions.

One significant aspect of regional dynamics is the border and territorial disputes between Kyrgyzstan and its neighbors. These disputes often revolve around issues such as water resources, access to transportation routes, and ethnic tensions. Diplomats must know these disputes and work towards peaceful resolutions that maintain regional stability.

Another crucial factor influencing regional dynamics is the economic foreign policy of Kyrgyzstan. The country is strategically interested in developing economic ties with its neighbors to boost trade and investment opportunities. Kyrgyzstan's membership in the Eurasian Economic Union (EAEU) and its participation in regional initiatives, such as the Belt and Road Initiative, demonstrates its commitment to regional economic integration.

Furthermore, Kyrgyzstan's security foreign policy is closely intertwined with its regional dynamics. The country faces various security challenges, including the threat of terrorism, drug trafficking, and ethnic conflicts. Cooperation with its neighbors and international partners is crucial in addressing these security concerns effectively. Diplomats must engage in dialogue and foster partnerships to promote regional security and stability.

In addition to these dynamics, Kyrgyzstan maintains cultural and educational foreign policies that foster cultural exchanges and cooperation with its regional counterparts. These policies aim to strengthen people-to-people ties and promote mutual understanding among the diverse ethnic groups in the region.

Overall, understanding the regional dynamics in Kyrgyzstan is essential for diplomats navigating the foreign policy landscape of the five "Tan" ex-Soviet republics. By recognizing the significance of border disputes, economic integration, security cooperation, cultural exchanges, and educational partnerships, diplomats can effectively engage with Kyrgyzstan and its neighbors to promote peace, stability, and economic prosperity in the region.

Regional Dynamics in Tajikistan

Tajikistan, located in Central Asia, is a key player in the regional dynamics of the five "Tan" ex-Soviet republics. This subchapter will delve into the various aspects of Tajikistan's foreign policy and its impact on the region, specifically focusing on its regional foreign policy.

As a landlocked country, Tajikistan faces unique challenges in terms of its regional dynamics. The country shares borders with Afghanistan, Uzbekistan, Kyrgyzstan, and China, making it strategically important for regional stability. Tajikistan's foreign policy aims to maintain good relations with its neighbors while safeguarding its national interests.

One of the key elements of Tajikistan's regional foreign policy is its focus on addressing security concerns. With the threat of terrorism and extremism emanating from neighboring Afghanistan, Tajikistan has actively engaged in regional security initiatives. It has cooperated with other countries in the region, such as Uzbekistan and Kyrgyzstan, to combat terrorism, drug trafficking, and transnational organized crime. Additionally, Tajikistan has actively participated in the Shanghai Cooperation Organization (SCO), which is crucial in addressing regional security challenges.

Tajikistan's regional foreign policy is economically centered on enhancing trade and investment opportunities. The country has prioritized regional economic integration through initiatives like the Central Asia Regional Economic Cooperation (CAREC) program. Tajikistan has also worked towards improving connectivity in the region by participating in infrastructure projects like the CASA-1000 electricity transmission project, which aims to export surplus electricity to Afghanistan and Pakistan.

Tajikistan's regional foreign policy also involves addressing border and territorial disputes. The country has had longstanding border disputes with Kyrgyzstan and has actively engaged in diplomatic negotiations to find peaceful resolutions. Tajikistan aims to foster stability and strengthen regional cooperation by resolving these disputes.

Furthermore, Tajikistan's foreign policy includes diplomatic relations with major powers. The country maintains relations with Russia, China, and the United States, seeking their support in economic development, security, and regional stability.

In conclusion, Tajikistan's regional dynamics play a crucial role in shaping the foreign policy landscape of the five "Tan" ex-Soviet republics. Through its regional foreign policy, Tajikistan aims to address security concerns, enhance economic cooperation, resolve border disputes, and engage with major powers. By navigating these dynamics effectively, Tajikistan contributes to regional stability and development in Central Asia.

Regional Dynamics in Turkmenistan

Turkmenistan, one of the five "Tan" ex-Soviet republics, is a country that holds significant regional dynamics within Central Asia. Understanding these dynamics is crucial for diplomats navigating the foreign policy landscape of the region.

Geographically, Turkmenistan shares borders with Kazakhstan, Uzbekistan, Afghanistan, and Iran, positioning it as a key player in regional affairs. Its strategic location allows it to influence and be influenced by the dynamics of its neighboring countries.

One important aspect of regional dynamics in Turkmenistan is its economic foreign policy. The country possesses vast reserves of natural gas, making it a significant energy exporter in the region. Its economic policies have focused on attracting foreign investment and diversifying its economy beyond the energy sector. Diplomats need to understand the economic priorities of Turkmenistan and explore avenues for collaboration and trade.

Energy foreign policy is another crucial area to consider. Turkmenistan has actively engaged in energy diplomacy, seeking to establish reliable energy routes and partnerships. The country's ambitious projects, such as the Turkmenistan-Afghanistan-Pakistan-India (TAPI) gas pipeline, aim to strengthen regional energy cooperation and enhance its geopolitical influence.

Security foreign policy is also a vital aspect of regional dynamics in Turkmenistan. The country has been committed to maintaining stability within its borders and the broader Central Asian region. Turkmenistan's neutrality and non-interference principles have allowed it to navigate the complex security challenges in the region while actively participating in regional security initiatives.

Moreover, Turkmenistan's regional foreign policy is characterized by its commitment to fostering good relations with its neighbors. Diplomats should understand the country's approach to regional integration and cooperation, which includes participation in regional organizations like the Commonwealth of Independent States (CIS) and the Shanghai Cooperation Organization (SCO).

Additionally, Turkmenistan's cultural and educational foreign policy plays a significant role in shaping regional dynamics. The country promotes cultural exchange and educational programs to enhance people-to-people connections and foster mutual understanding among the Central Asian nations.

In conclusion, diplomats engaging with Turkmenistan must be well-versed in the country's regional dynamics. Understanding its economic, energy, security, regional, cultural, and educational foreign policies is key to navigating the complexities of the Central Asian region. By fostering strong diplomatic relations and partnerships, diplomats can contribute to regional stability, economic development, and cooperation among the "Tan" ex-Soviet republics.

Regional Dynamics in Uzbekistan

Uzbekistan, one of the five "Tan" ex-Soviet republics, plays a crucial role in shaping the regional dynamics of Central Asia. This subchapter will explore the various aspects of Uzbekistan's regional foreign policy, highlighting its impact on neighboring countries and the wider region.

The principles of sovereignty, non-interference, and mutual respect guide Uzbekistan's foreign policy approach. As a landlocked country, its regional dynamics revolve around enhancing connectivity, promoting economic cooperation, and addressing security concerns.

Regarding economic foreign policy, Uzbekistan has actively pursued regional integration initiatives, such as the Central Asia Regional Economic Cooperation program. By fostering trade and investment ties with its neighbors, Uzbekistan aims to create a favorable business environment and stimulate economic growth in the region. The country's vast energy reserves also contribute to its role in shaping the energy foreign policy of Central Asia, as it seeks to diversify its energy exports and establish strategic partnerships with regional and international players.

Security is a key concern for Uzbekistan, given the volatile nature of the region. The country actively participates in regional security frameworks like the Shanghai Cooperation Organization to address common threats like terrorism, extremism, and drug trafficking.

Uzbekistan's efforts in this regard contribute to its own stability and have a significant impact on the security foreign policy of the entire Central Asian region.

Uzbekistan's regional foreign policy also extends to cultural and educational exchanges. By promoting cultural diplomacy and educational partnerships, the country aims to enhance people-to-people contacts and foster mutual understanding among the Central Asian nations. This approach aligns with Uzbekistan's broader goal of strengthening regional cooperation and promoting a sense of shared identity.

In conclusion, its economic, energy, security, cultural, and educational foreign policies shape Uzbekistan's regional dynamics. With its strategic location and proactive approach, Uzbekistan is crucial in fostering regional integration, addressing security challenges, and promoting cultural exchange in Central Asia. As diplomats, it is crucial to understand and engage with these dynamics to navigate the foreign policy landscape of the "Tan" ex-Soviet republics effectively.

Chapter 6: Cultural and Educational Foreign Policy

Cultural Exchange Programs in Kazakhstan

In foreign policy, cultural exchange programs foster understanding and build strong relationships between nations. Kazakhstan, one of the five "Tan" ex-Soviet republics, recognizes the significance of such programs and has actively engaged in various initiatives to promote cultural and educational exchange.

Kazakhstan's cultural exchange programs are designed to showcase the country's rich heritage and diversity while facilitating the exchange of ideas and knowledge. These programs strengthen diplomatic ties, enhance mutual understanding, and encourage collaboration in various fields.

One of the key platforms for cultural exchange in Kazakhstan is the International Cultural Festival, which brings together artists, performers, and cultural enthusiasts from different countries. This festival provides a unique opportunity for diplomats to experience Kazakhstan's vibrant arts and culture scene, including traditional music, dance, and cuisine. It also serves as a platform for artists to showcase their talents and promote cultural diversity.

In addition to festivals, Kazakhstan actively participates in student exchange programs with universities worldwide. These programs enable young diplomats to study in Kazakhstan and vice versa, fostering cross-cultural understanding and building long-lasting relationships. Diplomats gain insights into Kazakhstan's education system, traditions, and values through these exchanges while sharing their experiences and knowledge.

Kazakhstan also hosts international conferences and seminars on various topics, providing a platform for diplomats to engage in intellectual discussions and exchange ideas. These events cover various subjects, including economics, energy, security, and regional cooperation. Diplomats can network with experts, policymakers, and scholars, facilitating the exchange of perspectives and fostering collaborative solutions to common challenges.

Furthermore, Kazakhstan actively encourages cultural diplomacy by establishing cultural centers and institutes. These institutions promote language learning, cultural events, and academic exchanges, serving as hubs for diplomats to engage with Kazakhstan's cultural heritage.

Cultural exchange programs in Kazakhstan are vital for establishing strong diplomatic ties and promoting mutual understanding. They contribute to the overall foreign policy objectives of the country, including economic development, energy cooperation, and regional stability. By embracing cultural exchange, Kazakhstan is committed to fostering positive international relations and building bridges between nations.

In conclusion, cultural exchange programs in Kazakhstan play a significant role in the country's foreign policy landscape. These programs provide a platform for diplomats to engage in meaningful interactions, promote understanding, and strengthen ties between nations. Kazakhstan's commitment to cultural diplomacy reflects its desire to foster collaboration and build enduring partnerships in the global arena.

Cultural Exchange Programs in Kyrgyzstan

In foreign policy, cultural exchange programs hold immense value as they facilitate a deeper understanding and appreciation of a country's rich heritage, traditions, and way of life. Kyrgyzstan, one of the five

"Tan" ex-Soviet republics, has actively embraced cultural exchange programs to enhance diplomatic relations and promote its unique cultural identity on the global stage.

With its stunning landscapes, nomadic traditions, and vibrant arts and crafts, Kyrgyzstan offers an enriching experience for diplomats engaging in cultural exchange programs. These programs foster mutual understanding and build lasting relationships between Kyrgyzstan and other nations.

One such popular initiative is the Kyrgyz Cultural Ambassador Program. This program allows diplomats to immerse themselves in the country's diverse cultural landscape by participating in traditional music and dance performances, attending local festivals, and exploring historical sites. This firsthand experience allows diplomats to understand Kyrgyz culture comprehensively, enabling them to represent their own countries more effectively in diplomatic interactions.

Furthermore, Kyrgyzstan has also been actively involved in hosting international cultural festivals and exhibitions. These events provide a platform for cultural exchange, where diplomats can witness the richness and diversity of Kyrgyz arts, crafts, and traditions. The annual Nomad Games, for instance, showcase traditional sports and competitions, offering diplomats a unique opportunity to witness the nomadic heritage of the Kyrgyz people.

Cultural exchange programs also extend beyond traditional arts and crafts. The Kyrgyz government has proactively promoted educational exchanges, encouraging students and scholars from various countries to study and conduct research in Kyrgyzstan. This exchange of knowledge and ideas enhances diplomatic relations and contributes to the development of intellectual capital in both Kyrgyzstan and the participating nations.

Diplomats can contribute to the broader foreign policy goals by actively engaging in cultural exchange programs. These programs strengthen diplomatic ties and foster mutual respect and appreciation among nations. Diplomats can effectively navigate the foreign policy landscape and build enduring partnerships in trade, investment, security, and regional cooperation through a deeper understanding of Kyrgyzstan's cultural heritage.

In conclusion, cultural exchange programs in Kyrgyzstan play a vital role in shaping the foreign policy landscape of the country. By embracing and promoting its rich cultural heritage, Kyrgyzstan can forge stronger diplomatic relations, enhance its international standing, and create a platform for fruitful collaborations with other nations. As diplomats engage in these programs, they gain a deeper understanding of Kyrgyz culture, enabling them to foster meaningful dialogues and contribute to the broader goals of diplomacy in the five "Tan" ex-Soviet republics.

Cultural Exchange Programs in Tajikistan

Introduction:

As diplomats navigate the foreign policy landscape of the five "Tan" ex-Soviet republics, including Tajikistan, it is crucial to understand the significance of cultural exchange programs. These programs are vital in fostering mutual understanding, promoting diplomacy, and strengthening bilateral relations between countries. Tajikistan, a country rich in history, traditions, and cultural heritage, offers a unique opportunity for diplomats to engage in cultural exchange programs. This subchapter explores the importance and impact of such programs in Tajikistan.

Promoting Cultural Understanding:

Cultural exchange programs in Tajikistan provide diplomats with a platform to immerse themselves in the country's vibrant culture, traditions, and customs. By participating in these programs, diplomats gain a deeper understanding of Tajikistan's rich history, arts, music, and literature. This knowledge helps foster cultural understanding and enables diplomats to engage with Tajik counterparts and build stronger diplomatic ties effectively.

Enhancing Diplomatic Relations:

Cultural exchange programs serve as a bridge between nations, fostering people-to-people connections that contribute to enhanced diplomatic relations. Through these programs, diplomats can showcase their country's culture and values, promoting a positive image and strengthening bilateral ties. Furthermore, by interacting with Tajik artists, intellectuals, and scholars, diplomats can explore potential areas of collaboration, such as joint cultural projects or academic exchanges.

Preserving Cultural Heritage:

Tajikistan boasts a rich cultural heritage, including UNESCO World Heritage sites, ancient traditions, and unique art forms. Cultural exchange programs allow diplomats to appreciate and contribute to preserving Tajikistan's cultural heritage. Engaging in cultural festivals, exhibitions, and workshops enables diplomats to support the conservation of Tajik traditions and foster dialogue on cultural preservation.

Promoting Soft Power:

Cultural exchange programs in Tajikistan allow diplomats to harness the power of cultural diplomacy. Diplomats can promote their nation's soft power and influence by showcasing their country's artistic achievements, literature, cinema, and performing arts. This facilitates a deeper understanding of their own country and enhances its image and influence in Tajik society.

Conclusion:

Cultural exchange programs in Tajikistan provide diplomats a unique opportunity to engage in cultural diplomacy, foster mutual understanding, and strengthen bilateral relations. By immersing themselves in Tajikistan's rich culture, diplomats can enhance their diplomatic efforts, preserve cultural heritage, promote soft power, and contribute to the overall foreign policy objectives of the five "Tan" ex-Soviet republics. Embracing cultural exchange programs as a part of their diplomatic toolkit, diplomats can navigate the foreign policy landscape with a deeper understanding and appreciation of Tajikistan's cultural diversity.

Cultural Exchange Programs in Turkmenistan

Turkmenistan, one of the five "Tan" ex-Soviet republics, has been actively engaged in cultural exchange programs to promote its rich heritage and foster international understanding. These programs are crucial in shaping the country's foreign policy and enhancing its relations with other nations. This subchapter delves into Turkmenistan's cultural and educational foreign policy, highlighting the significance of cultural exchange programs in promoting diplomacy and mutual cooperation.

Turkmenistan, with its diverse ethnic groups and ancient civilizations, offers a wealth of cultural experiences for diplomats and international visitors. The country has recognized the value of cultural diplomacy in building bridges and fostering positive relations. Through cultural exchange programs, Turkmenistan aims to showcase its cultural treasures, traditions, and customs while embracing other nations' cultural diversity.

One of the key objectives of cultural exchange programs in Turkmenistan is to promote mutual understanding and respect. These programs allow diplomats to immerse themselves in Turkmen culture, arts, music, and literature. By participating in traditional festivals, art exhibitions, and cultural performances, diplomats can gain a deeper appreciation for the country's customs and traditions, fostering stronger diplomatic ties.

Furthermore, cultural exchange programs serve as a platform for Turkmenistan to showcase its achievements in various fields, such as education, science, and technology. The country's universities and research institutions actively collaborate, host international conferences, and facilitate student exchanges. These initiatives not only enhance educational standards but also contribute to the nation's overall development.

Turkmenistan also recognizes the importance of cultural diplomacy in promoting tourism and attracting foreign investment. The country aims to attract visitors and investors worldwide by showcasing its cultural heritage and natural beauty. Cultural exchange programs are vital in promoting Turkmenistan as a tourist destination and encouraging foreign businesses to invest in the country's economy.

In conclusion, cultural exchange programs are integral to Turkmenistan's foreign policy efforts. By promoting its cultural heritage, fostering mutual understanding, and attracting international visitors, Turkmenistan aims to strengthen diplomatic ties and foster cooperation with other nations. These programs contribute to the overall growth and development of the country, both economically and diplomatically. As diplomats navigate the foreign policy landscape of the five "Tan" ex-Soviet republics, understanding the significance of cultural exchange programs in Turkmenistan is crucial for building fruitful relationships and promoting cooperation.

Cultural Exchange Programs in Uzbekistan

In foreign policy, cultural exchange programs are vital in fostering understanding, building relationships, and promoting mutual respect between nations. Uzbekistan, one of the five "Tan" ex-Soviet republics, has recognized the significance of cultural and educational foreign policy in shaping its international relations. This subchapter explores the cultural exchange programs in Uzbekistan and their impact on the nation's diplomatic landscape.

Uzbekistan's cultural exchange programs showcase the country's rich heritage, traditions, and arts. These programs serve as a platform for diplomats and foreign officials to experience the country's vibrant cultural scene, fostering a deeper appreciation for Uzbekistan's unique identity. Through various initiatives, Uzbekistan aims to enhance its soft power, strengthen diplomatic ties, and promote its national interests abroad.

One of the flagship programs is the "Uzbekistan Cultural Diplomacy Initiative," which invites diplomats worldwide to immerse themselves in the country's cultural offerings. Participants engage in various activities, including visits to historical sites, museums, and art exhibitions and attending traditional music and dance performances. This program introduces foreign diplomats to Uzbekistan's cultural treasures and provides a platform for meaningful dialogue and understanding.

Additionally, Uzbekistan hosts numerous cultural festivals and events throughout the year, attracting artists, musicians, and performers from across the globe. These festivals bridge intercultural exchange, allowing diplomats to engage with their counterparts and local communities. The annual "Silk and Spices Festival" and the "Sharq Taronalari" (Melodies of the East) International Music Festival are two prominent events that showcase Uzbekistan's cultural diversity and artistic prowess.

Furthermore, Uzbekistan actively participates in cultural exchange programs with other nations, contributing to the global dialogue on cultural diplomacy. The country collaborates with international organizations, such as UNESCO, to preserve and promote its cultural heritage. Uzbekistan also engages in bilateral cultural agreements, facilitating the exchange of artists, scholars, and students with partner countries.

The cultural exchange programs in Uzbekistan strengthen diplomatic ties and contribute to the country's economic development. Promoting Uzbekistan's cultural heritage attracts tourists and boosts the local economy, generating employment opportunities and fostering sustainable growth.

In conclusion, Uzbekistan's cultural exchange programs are crucial in shaping its foreign policy landscape. These programs serve as a bridge between nations, fostering understanding and promoting the country's cultural identity. By actively engaging in cultural diplomacy, Uzbekistan aims to strengthen diplomatic ties, boost its soft power, and contribute to its economic development.

Chapter 7: Trade and Investment Foreign Policy

Trade Policies and Initiatives in Kazakhstan

Kazakhstan, one of the five "Tan" ex-Soviet republics, has made significant strides in developing its trade policies and initiatives to promote economic growth and attract foreign investment. As a diplomat navigating the foreign policy landscape of Kazakhstan, it is crucial to understand the country's approach to trade and the initiatives it has undertaken to enhance its economic foreign policy.

With its vast reserves of natural resources and strategic geographic location, Kazakhstan has positioned itself as a key player in the global trade arena. The country has implemented various trade policies and initiatives to foster economic cooperation and diversify its export markets.

One of the notable initiatives is the establishment of the Astana International Financial Center (AIFC), which serves as a financial hub for Central Asia and the wider region. The AIFC offers a business-friendly environment, with its legal system based on English common law and a regulatory framework aligned with international best practices. This initiative has attracted foreign investors and multinational corporations, facilitating trade and investment flows into Kazakhstan.

In addition, Kazakhstan has actively pursued regional integration through its membership in the Eurasian Economic Union (EAEU). The EAEU, comprising Russia, Belarus, Armenia, Kyrgyzstan, and Kazakhstan, aims to create a common market and promote economic cooperation among its member states. Through the EAEU, Kazakhstan has access to a larger market of over 180 million consumers and benefits from preferential trade agreements with other member countries.

Furthermore, Kazakhstan has been actively engaged in bilateral and multilateral trade negotiations to expand its market access and promote trade liberalization. The country has signed free trade agreements with countries such as China, the European Union, and the United States. These agreements have reduced trade barriers, facilitated the movement of goods and services, and provided a framework for resolving trade disputes.

Moreover, Kazakhstan has invested in infrastructure development to improve its connectivity and enhance trade facilitation. The country has developed transportation corridors, such as the Western Europe-Western China International Transit Corridor and the Trans-Caspian International Transport Route, to provide efficient and cost-effective transportation options for trade.

In conclusion, Kazakhstan has implemented various trade policies and initiatives to promote economic growth and attract foreign investment. The establishment of the AIFC, membership in the EAEU, and engagement in bilateral and multilateral trade negotiations are some of the key strategies employed by Kazakhstan to enhance its economic foreign policy. As a diplomat, understanding these trade policies and initiatives is crucial for navigating the foreign policy landscape of Kazakhstan and fostering strong diplomatic relations with the country.

Trade Policies and Initiatives in Kyrgyzstan

Trade plays a crucial role in the foreign policy of Kyrgyzstan, as it seeks to strengthen its economy and build partnerships with other nations. This subchapter explores Kyrgyzstan's trade policies and initiatives, focusing on its efforts to enhance economic cooperation and promote international trade.

As one of the five "Tan" ex-Soviet republics, Kyrgyzstan recognizes the importance of trade in fostering economic growth and development. The country has implemented various trade policies and initiatives to attract foreign investment, increase exports, and diversify its economy.

Kyrgyzstan has actively engaged in regional and international trade agreements to facilitate international trade. The country is a member of the Eurasian Economic Union (EAEU), which promotes economic integration and facilitates trade among its member states. Through the EAEU, Kyrgyzstan has gained access to a larger market, expanding its export opportunities and attracting foreign investments.

Furthermore, Kyrgyzstan has also pursued bilateral trade agreements with other countries to enhance economic cooperation. The country has signed agreements with neighboring countries such as Kazakhstan, Tajikistan, and Uzbekistan to promote trade and remove trade barriers. These agreements aim to streamline customs procedures, reduce tariffs, and facilitate the movement of goods across borders.

Kyrgyzstan has also focused on diversifying its economy by developing agriculture, textiles, and tourism sectors. The government has implemented policies to support these sectors, including providing incentives for investment, improving infrastructure, and promoting sustainable development practices. These initiatives aim to attract foreign investors and increase the country's export potential.

In addition to its trade policies, Kyrgyzstan has actively participated in international trade fairs and exhibitions to showcase its products and attract foreign buyers. The country has also established trade promotion agencies to facilitate business matchmaking and support exporters.

Kyrgyzstan's trade policies and initiatives demonstrate its commitment to enhancing economic cooperation and promoting international trade. By actively engaging in regional and international trade agreements, diversifying its economy, and participating in trade promotion activities, Kyrgyzstan aims to strengthen its position in the global market and attract foreign investments. These efforts contribute to the country's overall foreign policy objectives of achieving economic growth, stability, and regional integration.

Trade Policies and Initiatives in Tajikistan

Tajikistan, a landlocked country in Central Asia, has been developing its trade policies and initiatives to promote economic growth and attract foreign investment. This subchapter will provide an overview of Tajikistan's trade policies and initiatives, highlighting the key areas of focus and the challenges faced by the country in this regard.

One of the main objectives of Tajikistan's trade policies is to diversify its export markets and reduce its dependence on a few commodities. The country has been actively seeking to expand its trade relations with traditional partners, such as Russia and China, as well as non-traditional markets in the Middle East and South Asia. Tajikistan has been negotiating and signing various bilateral and regional free trade agreements to achieve this. These agreements aim to reduce trade barriers, facilitate the movement of goods and services, and enhance market access for Tajikistani exporters.

In addition to bilateral agreements, Tajikistan has actively participated in regional trade initiatives. The country is a member of the Eurasian Economic Union (EAEU), a regional economic bloc comprising several former Soviet republics. This membership has provided Tajikistan access to a larger market and facilitated trade with other EAEU member states. Furthermore, Tajikistan is also a member of the World Trade Organization (WTO), which has helped the country to improve its trade regulations and standards in line with international norms.

Despite these efforts, Tajikistan faces several trade policies and initiatives challenges. One of the major challenges is the lack of infrastructure, including transportation networks and customs facilities, which hinders trade facilitation and increases transaction costs. Tajikistan has been working to address these infrastructure constraints by investing in developing transport corridors, including the Central Asia Regional Economic Cooperation (CAREC) program.

Another challenge is the country's heavy reliance on remittances from migrant workers, which accounts for a significant portion of its GDP. This reliance on remittances makes Tajikistan vulnerable to external shocks and economic downturns. To reduce this vulnerability, Tajikistan has focused on diversifying its economy and promoting non-traditional exports, such as textiles, agro-processing, and tourism.

In conclusion, Tajikistan's trade policies and initiatives aim to diversify its export markets, reduce dependence on a few commodities, and attract foreign investment. The country is actively engaged in bilateral and regional trade agreements and participating in international trade organizations. However, challenges such as infrastructure constraints and reliance on remittances need to be addressed to realize the potential of Tajikistan's trade sector fully. Diplomats involved in the foreign policy of the five "Tan" ex-Soviet republics should consider these trade policies and initiatives when engaging with Tajikistan, as they play a crucial role in the country's economic development and overall foreign policy objectives.

Trade Policies and Initiatives in Turkmenistan

Introduction:

In recent years, Turkmenistan has implemented various trade policies and initiatives to enhance its economic growth and promote international trade relations. This subchapter will provide an overview of Turkmenistan's trade policies and initiatives, highlighting the country's efforts to attract foreign investments, diversify its economy, and expand its trade partnerships.

Attracting Foreign Investments:

Turkmenistan has made significant efforts to attract foreign direct investments (FDIs) by implementing favorable trade policies and creating a business-friendly environment. The government has established special economic zones and industrial parks, offering tax incentives and streamlined administrative procedures to foreign investors. These initiatives encourage foreign companies to invest in key sectors such as energy, agriculture, telecommunications, and infrastructure development.

Diversifying the Economy:

Turkmenistan has prioritized diversifying its economy through trade policies focused on non-oil sectors to reduce its dependence on hydrocarbon exports. The government has implemented measures to promote industries such as textiles, agriculture, manufacturing, and tourism. By encouraging the development of these sectors, Turkmenistan aims to strengthen its domestic production capabilities, create employment opportunities, and reduce its reliance on imported goods.

Expanding Trade Partnerships:

Turkmenistan has actively pursued trade partnerships with both regional and global players. The country has engaged in various multilateral trade agreements, including the World Trade Organization (WTO) accession process. Turkmenistan has also strengthened its economic ties within the Central Asian region by establishing the Commonwealth of Independent States (CIS) Free Trade Area.

Furthermore, the government has actively pursued bilateral trade agreements with countries such as China, Russia, Turkey, and the European Union, facilitating the exchange of goods, services, and investments.

Trade Facilitation Measures:

To enhance its trade competitiveness, Turkmenistan has implemented several trade facilitation measures. These include simplifying customs procedures, reducing trade barriers, and improving infrastructure connectivity. The country has invested in modernizing its transportation networks, including developing new ports, railways, and highways, to facilitate the movement of goods across borders. Additionally, Turkmenistan has implemented electronic customs systems and adopted international trade standards to streamline trade processes and enhance transparency.

Conclusion:

Turkmenistan's trade policies and initiatives reflect its commitment to fostering economic growth, attracting foreign investments, and diversifying its economy. By actively engaging in global and regional trade partnerships, Turkmenistan aims to strengthen its position in the international market and expand its export opportunities. The government's efforts to simplify trade procedures and improve infrastructure connectivity demonstrate its commitment to facilitating trade and promoting a business-friendly environment. As Turkmenistan continues to pursue its economic development goals, implementing effective trade policies and initiatives will remain crucial to its long-term success.

Trade Policies and Initiatives in Uzbekistan

Uzbekistan has made significant strides in recent years to develop and implement trade policies and initiatives that promote economic growth and enhance its position in the global marketplace. As a key player in the Central Asian region, the country has recognized the importance of trade to stimulate domestic industries, attract foreign investment, and strengthen diplomatic relations with major powers.

One of Uzbekistan's key trade policies is the export market diversification. The government has actively sought to expand its trading partners beyond traditional markets, such as Russia and China, by exploring new opportunities in Europe, the Middle East, and Southeast Asia. This strategy has not only helped to reduce dependence on a limited number of countries but has also opened up avenues for Uzbek businesses to access larger consumer markets.

Uzbekistan has implemented various initiatives to improve its business environment and enhance trade logistics to facilitate trade. These initiatives include streamlining customs procedures, reducing bureaucratic red tape, and investing in modern infrastructure and transportation networks. The country has also actively participated in regional integration efforts, such as the Eurasian Economic Union and the Shanghai Cooperation Organization, to promote trade liberalization and facilitate cross-border trade.

Furthermore, Uzbekistan has strongly emphasised attracting foreign direct investment (FDI) to stimulate economic growth and promote technological transfer. The government has implemented policies to create an investor-friendly climate, including tax incentives, simplified licensing procedures, and establishment of special economic zones. These initiatives have increased FDI inflows, particularly in energy, manufacturing, and agriculture sectors.

Regarding trade promotion, Uzbekistan has actively participated in international trade fairs and exhibitions to showcase its products and attract foreign buyers. The government has also established trade missions abroad and engaged in bilateral and multilateral negotiations to secure preferential trade agreements and expand market access for its exporters.

Overall, Uzbekistan's trade policies and initiatives have significantly driven economic growth and diversification. Uzbekistan has positioned itself as a regional trade hub and a key player in the global marketplace by actively pursuing new markets, improving trade logistics, attracting foreign investment, and promoting its products abroad. As such, diplomats engaging with Uzbekistan must be well-versed in these trade policies and initiatives to effectively navigate the country's foreign policy landscape and explore opportunities for collaboration and partnership.

Chapter 8: International Alliances and Partnerships

Multilateral Engagements of Kazakhstan

Kazakhstan, one of the five "Tan" ex-Soviet republics, has pursued a multifaceted approach to its foreign policy, engaging in various multilateral initiatives and partnerships. This subchapter will explore the key multilateral engagements of Kazakhstan and their significance in shaping its foreign policy landscape.

First and foremost, Kazakhstan has actively participated in regional organizations such as the Shanghai Cooperation Organization (SCO) and the Eurasian Economic Union (EAEU). The SCO, comprising countries from Central Asia and beyond, has provided a platform for Kazakhstan to enhance regional security cooperation, combat terrorism, and promote economic integration. Similarly, the EAEU has facilitated Kazakhstan's economic integration with its neighboring states, fostering trade and investment opportunities.

Kazakhstan has also been an active member of international alliances and partnerships. Notably, it has been a non-permanent member of the United Nations Security Council, playing a crucial role in global peacekeeping efforts and advocating for the interests of the Central Asian region. Additionally, Kazakhstan has been a member of the Organization for Security and Cooperation in Europe (OSCE), contributing to conflict resolution and promoting human rights within the region.

Regarding regional foreign policy, Kazakhstan has pursued initiatives to foster stability and cooperation in Central Asia. The country has significantly mediated border and territorial disputes among its neighbors, promoting dialogue and peaceful resolutions. Moreover,

Kazakhstan has actively engaged in cultural and educational exchanges to enhance understanding and cooperation among nations.

Economically, Kazakhstan has leveraged its energy resources to become a key player in the global energy market. Kazakhstan has developed strategic partnerships with various countries through the Caspian Sea region, ensuring energy security and diversification. Additionally, Kazakhstan's trade and investment foreign policy has focused on attracting foreign direct investment and expanding its export markets, particularly in agriculture, mining, and manufacturing sectors.

While Kazakhstan has made significant progress in its multilateral engagements, challenges remain. The country continues to navigate diplomatic relations with major powers, balancing its alignment with Russia, China, and the West. Furthermore, human rights and democracy promotion remain areas of concern, with Kazakhstan facing scrutiny over its record.

In conclusion, Kazakhstan's multilateral engagements are vital in shaping its foreign policy landscape. Kazakhstan seeks to promote regional stability, foster economic development, and enhance its global standing through active participation in regional organisations, international alliances, and partnerships. However, the country faces ongoing challenges, particularly in balancing its relationships with major powers and addressing human rights concerns.

Multilateral Engagements of Kyrgyzstan

Kyrgyzstan, one of the five "Tan" ex-Soviet republics, has actively engaged in multilateral diplomacy to strengthen its foreign policy objectives. This chapter examines Kyrgyzstan's multilateral engagements, including economic, energy, security, regional, cultural and educational, trade and investment, international alliances and partnerships, border and territorial disputes, diplomatic relations with major powers, and human rights and democracy promotion.

Regarding economic foreign policy, Kyrgyzstan has sought to diversify its economy and attract foreign investments. The country has actively participated in regional economic initiatives such as the Eurasian Economic Union (EEU) and the Shanghai Cooperation Organization (SCO). Kyrgyzstan has forged partnerships to enhance its trade, investment, and economic cooperation with other member states through these platforms.

Kyrgyzstan's energy foreign policy focuses on harnessing its vast hydroelectric potential. The country has engaged in regional energy projects, including constructing hydropower plants and developing regional power grids. Kyrgyzstan aims to ensure energy security and contribute to the regional energy market by promoting energy cooperation.

Regarding security foreign policy, Kyrgyzstan has actively participated in regional security organizations such as the Collective Security Treaty Organization (CSTO) and the SCO. The country has collaborated with other member states to combat terrorism, drug trafficking, and other transnational threats. Furthermore, Kyrgyzstan has hosted joint military exercises and conferences to enhance regional security cooperation.

Kyrgyzstan's regional foreign policy emphasizes its role as a bridge between Central Asia, Russia, and China. The country has actively promoted regional integration and connectivity through the Belt and Road Initiative (BRI) and the Central Asia Regional Economic Cooperation (CAREC) program. By strengthening regional ties, Kyrgyzstan aims to enhance economic development, stability, and cooperation in Central Asia.

Regarding cultural and educational foreign policy, Kyrgyzstan has focused on promoting its rich cultural heritage and educational opportunities. The country has organized various cultural exchange programs, festivals, and exhibitions to showcase its traditional arts, music, and cuisine. Additionally, Kyrgyzstan has attracted international students through scholarships and educational partnerships, contributing to its human capital development.

Kyrgyzstan's trade and investment foreign policy aims to attract foreign direct investment and expand its export markets. The country has pursued trade agreements and preferential trade arrangements with various countries and regional blocs. Kyrgyzstan seeks to boost its economic growth and create employment opportunities by enhancing trade and investment.

Kyrgyzstan has also actively engaged in international alliances and partnerships to promote its foreign policy interests. The country has developed strategic partnerships with major powers such as Russia, China, and the United States. Through these partnerships, Kyrgyzstan aims to enhance its security, trade, and diplomatic relations on the global stage.

Regarding border and territorial disputes, Kyrgyzstan has been involved in ongoing negotiations and dialogue with neighboring countries to resolve outstanding issues. The country has sought peaceful and diplomatic solutions to border disputes, emphasizing the importance of maintaining regional stability and cooperation.

Regarding diplomatic relations with major powers, Kyrgyzstan has pursued a balanced approach, maintaining friendly relations with Russia, China, and the United States. The country has diversified its partnerships to protect its national interests while seeking mutually beneficial cooperation with major powers.

Finally, Kyrgyzstan has tried to promote human rights and democracy in its foreign policy. The country has engaged in international human rights organizations and initiatives, advocating for the protection of human rights and democratic values. Kyrgyzstan has also implemented domestic reforms to strengthen democracy, the rule of law, and good governance.

In conclusion, Kyrgyzstan's multilateral engagements in various aspects of foreign policy have played a crucial role in shaping its international relations. Through active participation in regional and international initiatives, Kyrgyzstan has sought to enhance its economic development, energy security, regional stability, cultural exchanges, trade and investment, strategic partnerships, border resolution, diplomatic relations, and the promotion of human rights and democracy. These engagements reflect Kyrgyzstan's commitment to actively navigate the foreign policy landscape of the five "Tan" ex-Soviet republics and contribute to regional and global cooperation.

Multilateral Engagements of Tajikistan

Tajikistan, one of the five "Tan" ex-Soviet republics, has actively engaged in multilateral initiatives to shape its foreign policy and strengthen its position on the global stage. This subchapter explores the various multilateral engagements of Tajikistan and their implications for its foreign policy.

One of the key aspects of Tajikistan's multilateral engagements is its active participation in regional organizations. Tajikistan is a member of the Shanghai Cooperation Organization (SCO), which aims to promote cooperation in security, economy, and culture among its member states. Tajikistan seeks to enhance regional security and stability through its involvement in the SCO, particularly in combating terrorism, drug trafficking, and transnational organized crime.

Additionally, Tajikistan is a member of the Commonwealth of Independent States (CIS), which fosters cooperation among post-Soviet states. The CIS provides a platform for Tajikistan to engage with its neighbors on various issues, including trade, economy, and cultural exchange.

Furthermore, Tajikistan actively participates in the United Nations (UN) and its specialized agencies. As a UN member state, Tajikistan contributes to global discussions and decision-making processes on sustainable development, climate change, and peacekeeping operations. Tajikistan's engagement with the UN helps to raise its profile and establish diplomatic relations with other countries.

Regarding economic multilateralism, Tajikistan is a member of the World Trade Organization (WTO), enabling it to benefit from a rules-based trading system and access international markets. Tajikistan's participation in the WTO has facilitated the growth of its trade and investment sector, attracting foreign direct investment and promoting economic development.

Tajikistan also engages in multilateral energy initiatives, particularly through its Central Asia Regional Economic Cooperation (CAREC) program membership. CAREC aims to enhance regional connectivity and cooperation in the energy sector, promoting energy infrastructure development and efficient use of energy resources.

In conclusion, Tajikistan's multilateral engagements play a crucial role in shaping its foreign policy and promoting its interests on the global stage. Tajikistan seeks to enhance security, economic cooperation, and cultural exchange through active participation in regional organizations, such as the SCO and CIS. Its involvement in international organizations like the UN and WTO enables it to contribute to global discussions and benefit from a rules-based trading system. Additionally, Tajikistan's engagement in multilateral energy initiatives helps to promote regional connectivity and the sustainable development of its energy resources. Tajikistan's multilateral engagements reflect its commitment to diplomacy and cooperation in addressing regional and global challenges.

Multilateral Engagements of Turkmenistan

Turkmenistan, one of the five "Tan" ex-Soviet republics, has pursued a multifaceted approach to its foreign policy, engaging in various multilateral platforms to further its national interests. This subchapter delves into the multilateral engagements of Turkmenistan, highlighting its efforts to foster regional cooperation, enhance economic ties, and promote cultural and educational exchanges.

Regarding regional foreign policy, Turkmenistan has actively participated in the Central Asian Cooperation Organization (CACO). Through this platform, Turkmenistan has sought to strengthen regional stability, foster economic integration, and promote dialogue among the Central Asian states. Turkmenistan's membership in CACO has allowed it to address common challenges, such as border security, terrorism, and drug trafficking, through joint initiatives and collaboration.

Economically, Turkmenistan has pursued an ambitious foreign policy strategy focused on energy cooperation. As a significant natural gas producer, Turkmenistan has sought to diversify its energy export routes and reduce dependence on a single market. Through initiatives like the Turkmenistan-Afghanistan-Pakistan-India (TAPI) gas pipeline, Turkmenistan aims to expand its energy exports to South Asia, opening up new markets and enhancing regional economic integration.

Furthermore, Turkmenistan has actively engaged in cultural and educational exchanges as part of its foreign policy agenda. The country has partnered with international organizations and foreign institutions to promote educational cooperation, student exchanges, and cultural programs. These initiatives foster mutual understanding, promote Turkmen culture abroad, and enhance people-to-people contacts.

Turkmenistan has also sought to build international alliances and partnerships to strengthen its position on the global stage. The country has actively engaged with major powers, such as Russia, China, and the European Union, to enhance economic ties, attract foreign investment, and explore new avenues for cooperation. Turkmenistan's strategic location and abundant natural resources make it an attractive partner for many countries seeking to expand their regional influence.

In conclusion, Turkmenistan's multilateral engagements have shaped its foreign policy agenda. Through active participation in regional organizations, the pursuit of economic cooperation, the promotion of cultural and educational exchanges, and the establishment of international alliances, Turkmenistan has sought to further its national interests and enhance its standing in the global arena. As diplomats navigating the foreign policy landscape of the "Tan" ex-Soviet republics, understanding Turkmenistan's multilateral engagements is essential for fostering effective relations and cooperation with this important Central Asian nation.

Multilateral Engagements of Uzbekistan

As one of the five "Tan" ex-Soviet republics, Uzbekistan has actively participated in multilateral engagements to shape its foreign policy landscape. This subchapter explores how Uzbekistan engages with the international community, focusing on its regional, cultural, and economic foreign policies.

Regarding regional foreign policy, Uzbekistan has been a key player in Central Asia. It has actively pursued regional cooperation through organizations such as the Shanghai Cooperation Organization (SCO) and the Central Asian Cooperation Organization (CACO). Through these platforms, Uzbekistan aims to enhance security, promote economic development, and address common challenges such as terrorism and drug trafficking.

Culturally and educationally, Uzbekistan has also engaged with the international community. The country has sought to promote its rich cultural heritage through initiatives such as the Silk Road Tourism Forum and the International Music Festival "Sharq Taronalari." Additionally, Uzbekistan has actively participated in educational exchanges and partnerships to foster academic collaboration and cultural understanding.

Economically, Uzbekistan has pursued an active foreign policy to attract foreign trade and investment. The country has implemented economic reforms to create a favorable business environment and has actively engaged with international organizations such as the World Bank and the International Monetary Fund. Uzbekistan's focus on diversifying its economy and attracting foreign investment has resulted in fruitful partnerships with countries such as China, Russia, and the European Union.

Furthermore, Uzbekistan has forged international alliances and partnerships to strengthen its position on the global stage. It has developed strategic partnerships with major powers such as the United States, Russia, and China while actively engaging with regional partners such as Kazakhstan, Kyrgyzstan, Tajikistan, and Turkmenistan.

In conclusion, Uzbekistan's multilateral engagements are crucial in shaping its foreign policy landscape. Uzbekistan has positioned itself as an active player in the international community through regional cooperation, cultural and educational initiatives, economic reforms, and strategic alliances. As diplomats navigating the foreign policy landscape of the five "Tan" ex-Soviet republics, it is essential to understand and appreciate the multifaceted nature of Uzbekistan's engagements to effectively engage with the country and promote mutual understanding and collaboration.

Chapter 9: Border and Territorial Disputes

Border Issues in Kazakhstan

Border issues play a crucial role in the foreign policy of Kazakhstan, as the nation shares a border with several neighboring countries, including Russia, China, Kyrgyzstan, Uzbekistan, and Turkmenistan. These border disputes significantly affect Kazakhstan's diplomatic relations, regional stability, and economic development.

One of the key border issues that Kazakhstan faces is the delimitation and demarcation of its borders with its neighbors. Since gaining independence from the Soviet Union, Kazakhstan has negotiated with these countries to clarify its territorial boundaries. These negotiations have been complex and, at times, contentious, as they involve determining the physical borders and addressing historical and ethnic factors.

For example, the border dispute with Kyrgyzstan stems from the Soviet era when arbitrary administrative borders were drawn without considering ethnic and cultural divisions. Kazakhstan and Kyrgyzstan have been working together to resolve these issues through bilateral negotiations and have made progress in recent years. However, challenges remain, particularly regarding the delineation of disputed enclaves and the rights of ethnic minorities residing along the border.

Another significant border concern for Kazakhstan is its relationship with China. The Kazakh-Chinese border extends over 1,700 kilometers and is one of the longest international borders in the world. Although the border has been largely peaceful, there have been occasional tensions, primarily related to illegal border crossings, smuggling, and natural resource disputes. Kazakhstan's foreign policy aims to maintain a balanced and cooperative relationship with China while safeguarding its national interests and territorial integrity.

Resolving these border issues is crucial for Kazakhstan's foreign policy objectives, as they directly impact regional stability, economic cooperation, and cross-border trade. Kazakhstan recognizes the importance of maintaining peaceful and mutually beneficial relations with its neighbors and has tried to strengthen diplomatic ties and engage in dialogue.

In conclusion, border issues in Kazakhstan are a significant aspect of its foreign policy landscape. The nation's diplomatic efforts are focused on resolving territorial disputes, clarifying boundaries, and promoting stability and cooperation with neighboring countries. By addressing these challenges, Kazakhstan seeks to create an environment conducive to economic development, regional integration, and the overall well-being of its citizens.

Border Issues in Kyrgyzstan

Border issues play a crucial role in shaping the foreign policy of Kyrgyzstan, a landlocked country in Central Asia. As diplomats navigating the foreign policy landscape of the five "Tan" ex-Soviet Republics, it is essential to understand the intricacies surrounding border and territorial disputes in Kyrgyzstan.

Kyrgyzstan shares borders with Kazakhstan, Tajikistan, Uzbekistan, and China, making it vulnerable to various challenges and complexities. Resolving these border disputes is vital for regional stability, economic development, and fostering diplomatic relations.

One of the significant border issues in Kyrgyzstan is the ongoing dispute with Tajikistan over the Ferghana Valley. This contentious area has been a source of tension between the two countries for decades, leading to occasional clashes and even casualties. Diplomats must work towards finding mutually acceptable solutions that respect the historical, cultural, and ethnic dynamics of the region.

Another border concern is the porous border with Uzbekistan. The lack of clear distinction in certain areas has resulted in smuggling, illicit trade, and cross-border criminal activities. Diplomats must prioritize border management initiatives, such as enhancing border control infrastructure, establishing joint border patrols, and promoting information sharing to combat these challenges effectively.

Furthermore, Kyrgyzstan faces border-related issues with China. The border between the two countries spans over 1,000 kilometers, and occasional disputes have occurred regarding territorial claims and resource exploration. Diplomats should engage in constructive dialogue with China to strengthen bilateral relations and resolve border-related conflicts peacefully.

Addressing these border issues requires a comprehensive approach considering historical, cultural, economic, and security factors. Diplomats should actively engage in diplomatic negotiations, mediation, and confidence-building measures to foster peaceful resolutions. Strengthening regional cooperation frameworks, such as the Shanghai Cooperation Organization (SCO), can also contribute to resolving these disputes.

In conclusion, border issues in Kyrgyzstan are crucial elements of its foreign policy landscape. Diplomats must be well-informed about the complexities surrounding these territorial disputes and work towards peaceful resolutions that promote regional stability, economic growth, and stronger diplomatic ties. By effectively addressing these border issues, Kyrgyzstan can foster an environment of trust, cooperation, and mutual understanding with its neighboring countries.

Border Issues in Tajikistan

Tajikistan, one of the five "Tan" ex-Soviet republics, faces numerous border issues that play a crucial role in its foreign policy. These border disputes significantly affect regional stability, economic development, and diplomatic relations. This subchapter aims to shed light on the border challenges faced by Tajikistan and explore their impact on its foreign policy.

Tajikistan shares borders with Afghanistan, Uzbekistan, Kyrgyzstan, and China, making it a strategically important nation. However, these borderlines have been a source of contention and dispute. The most significant border issue for Tajikistan is the boundary with Kyrgyzstan. The disputed areas primarily revolve around resource-rich territories and access to water resources, leading to tensions between the two countries. These disputes have occasionally escalated into violent clashes, threatening regional stability and hindering diplomatic relations.

Another significant border challenge is Tajikistan's porous border with Afghanistan. This poses a considerable security threat, particularly regarding the illegal drug trade and the movement of terrorist groups. Tajikistan has been working closely with its international partners, including Russia and the United States, to enhance border security and combat these challenges. The country's foreign policy emphasizes the need for regional cooperation and collaboration in addressing transnational threats.

Furthermore, Tajikistan's border with Uzbekistan has also witnessed sporadic tensions, primarily related to territorial claims and resource access. These disputes have directly impacted bilateral relations and hindered economic cooperation between the two nations. Tajikistan's foreign policy aims to establish peaceful and mutually beneficial relations with Uzbekistan, and resolving these border disputes is a crucial step towards achieving this goal.

In conclusion, border issues in Tajikistan play a significant role in shaping its foreign policy. These disputes impact regional stability, economic development, and diplomatic relations with neighboring countries. Tajikistan addresses these challenges diplomatically and seeks regional cooperation to ensure peaceful and mutually beneficial solutions. Resolving border disputes is vital for Tajikistan's overall foreign policy objectives, including regional integration, economic growth, and stability.

Border Issues in Turkmenistan

Border issues play a significant role in shaping the foreign policy of Turkmenistan, one of the five "Tan" ex-Soviet republics. This subchapter will delve into Turkmenistan's various border and territorial disputes, highlighting their impact on the country's diplomatic relations and regional stability.

Turkmenistan shares borders with Kazakhstan, Uzbekistan, Afghanistan, and Iran, making territorial integrity a crucial aspect of its foreign policy. One of the most contentious border disputes is with Uzbekistan, primarily centered around the boundary of the Amu Darya River. This dispute has led to occasional tensions and affected bilateral relations between the two countries.

Another significant border issue is the dispute with Iran over the Caspian Sea's delimitation. The Caspian Sea holds immense strategic and economic importance, particularly regarding energy resources. Turkmenistan's desire to exploit its offshore oil and gas reserves has often clashed with Iran's claims, resulting in a prolonged stalemate. Resolving this dispute is crucial for Turkmenistan's foreign energy policy and relations with Iran.

Furthermore, Turkmenistan faces challenges along its southern border with Afghanistan. The volatile security situation in Afghanistan has had spill-over effects, including drug trafficking and cross-border terrorism. Turkmenistan has been actively engaged in regional efforts to enhance border security, including cooperation with neighboring countries and international partners.

Addressing these border issues has been a priority for Turkmenistan's foreign policy. The country has pursued diplomatic means, engaging in negotiations and dialogue to find mutually acceptable solutions. Turkmenistan has also sought the involvement of international organizations and major powers to mediate and facilitate resolutions.

Stability and peaceful resolution of border disputes are essential for Turkmenistan's economic growth and regional integration. The country's foreign policy promotes regional cooperation and connectivity, and border issues pose significant challenges to achieving these objectives.

In conclusion, border issues in Turkmenistan have a profound impact on the country's foreign policy. The disputes with Uzbekistan and Iran and the security challenges along the Afghan border shape Turkmenistan's diplomatic relations and regional aspirations. Resolving these border disputes is crucial for Turkmenistan's stability, economic development, and the pursuit of regional cooperation. Diplomats engaged in the foreign policy of the five "Tan" ex-Soviet republics must navigate these complex issues to foster peace and prosperity in the region.

Border Issues in Uzbekistan

One of the key aspects of foreign policy in Uzbekistan is the management of border and territorial disputes. As a landlocked country in Central Asia, Uzbekistan shares borders with all four of its neighboring "Tan" ex-Soviet republics: Kazakhstan, Kyrgyzstan, Tajikistan, and Turkmenistan. These borders have been the subject of various conflicts and tensions, making border management a crucial component of Uzbekistan's foreign policy.

One prominent border issue in Uzbekistan is the Ferghana Valley, a densely populated and resource-rich region divided between Uzbekistan, Kyrgyzstan, and Tajikistan. The complex ethnic and historical dynamics in this region have led to periodic tensions and disputes over control and access to resources. Uzbekistan has been actively engaged in negotiations and dialogue with its neighbors to find peaceful resolutions to these border issues, recognizing the importance of stability and cooperation in the region.

Another significant border issue for Uzbekistan is the border with Afghanistan. The porous nature of this border has posed challenges in terms of cross-border security threats, including drug trafficking, terrorism, and illegal migration. Uzbekistan has been proactive in strengthening its border control measures, including the construction of physical barriers and the deployment of security forces, to address these challenges and safeguard its territorial integrity and national security.

Furthermore, the border with Turkmenistan has also presented some challenges for Uzbekistan. The demarcation of the border has been a contentious issue, particularly in the regions rich in natural resources. Uzbekistan has negotiated with Turkmenistan to resolve these disputes peacefully and ensure a mutually beneficial outcome for both countries.

Uzbekistan recognizes that effective border management is vital for promoting regional stability, economic cooperation, and security. As such, it actively participates in regional organizations such as the Shanghai Cooperation Organization (SCO) and the Central Asia Regional Economic Cooperation (CAREC) program to foster dialogue and collaboration with its neighbors on border issues.

In conclusion, border issues are significant in Uzbekistan's foreign policy. The country is committed to the peaceful resolution of territorial disputes, recognizing the importance of stability, security, and cooperation in the region. Uzbekistan seeks to promote a climate of trust and cooperation among its "Tan" ex-Soviet republic neighbors, fostering regional integration and development by actively engaging in negotiations and participating in regional organisations.

Chapter 10: Diplomatic Relations with Major Powers

Relations with Russia

Relations with Russia are crucial in the foreign policy of the five "Tan" ex-Soviet republics – Kazakhstan, Kyrgyzstan, Tajikistan, Turkmenistan, and Uzbekistan. These countries in Central Asia share historical, cultural, and economic ties with Russia, stemming from their shared Soviet past. As diplomats navigating the foreign policy landscape of these republics, it is essential to understand the dynamics of their relations with Russia and its implications for their respective national interests.

Historically, these republics have maintained close ties with Russia due to their geographical proximity and economic interdependence. Russia is a major trading partner and a primary source of investment for these countries, particularly in the energy sector. Additionally, many people in the region share ethnic and linguistic ties with Russia, further strengthening the bond between the two.

However, these relations have not been without challenges. The five "Tan" ex-Soviet republics have sought to balance their relations with Russia while asserting their national interests. They aspire to maintain their sovereignty and independence while benefiting from mutually advantageous partnerships with Russia.

One key aspect of the relationship is energy cooperation. The republics possess significant energy resources, and Russia has been a major consumer and transit country for their oil and gas exports. However, tensions have arisen as these countries have sought to diversify their export routes and reduce their dependence on Russia. Building alternative pipelines and seeking partnerships with other countries have been important strategies in achieving this goal.

Regarding security, the republics have collaborated with Russia through various regional organizations, such as the Collective Security Treaty Organization (CSTO). This cooperation addresses common security challenges, including terrorism, drug trafficking, and transnational organized crime. At the same time, the republics have pursued a delicate balance by engaging with other international actors, such as the United States and China, to diversify their security partnerships.

Furthermore, these republics maintain diplomatic relations with major powers, including the United States, China, and the European Union. They seek to leverage these relationships to promote national interests, attract foreign investment, and enhance regional standing. Balancing these ties with their relations with Russia is an ongoing challenge.

In conclusion, relations with Russia are important in the foreign policy of the five "Tan" ex-Soviet republics. While maintaining historical and economic ties, these countries strive to assert their independence, diversify their partnerships, and safeguard their national interests. As diplomats, understanding the nuances and complexities of these relations is vital for effectively navigating the foreign policy landscape of the region.

Relations with China

China plays a crucial role in the foreign policy landscape of the five "Tan" ex-Soviet republics - Kazakhstan, Kyrgyzstan, Tajikistan, Turkmenistan, and Uzbekistan. As diplomats navigating this complex terrain, understanding and effectively managing relations with China is paramount.

China's economic foreign policy has significant implications for the "Tan" republics. With its rapidly growing economy and vast market potential, China offers numerous opportunities for trade and investment. The "Tan" republics have actively engaged with China to enhance economic cooperation, attract investments, and tap into Chinese markets. Diplomats must foster strong economic ties with China to promote economic growth and development in their respective countries.

Energy is another crucial aspect of China's foreign policy. As a major consumer of energy resources, China's energy demands directly impact the "Tan" republics, which possess abundant reserves of oil, gas, and minerals. Diplomats should engage in energy diplomacy with China to ensure mutual benefits, including fair pricing, stable supply, and technology transfer.

Security cooperation with China is essential for the "Tan" republics to maintain regional stability and counter common security threats. Diplomats should work closely with China to address terrorism, separatism, and drug trafficking. Additionally, collaboration in military training, joint exercises, and information sharing can contribute to regional security.

China's influence in the region extends to its regional foreign policy. The "Tan" republics share borders with China, making them critical players in China's regional initiatives like the Belt and Road Initiative (BRI). Diplomats must navigate the complexities of the BRI, ensuring that their countries' interests are protected while maximizing the potential benefits of infrastructure development and regional connectivity.

Cultural and educational exchanges with China can foster people-to-people ties and promote mutual understanding. Diplomats should encourage cultural exchanges, scholarships, and academic collaborations to strengthen cultural and educational foreign policy with China.

Diplomats must also carefully manage diplomatic relations with major powers, including China, to maintain a balanced approach. Balancing between major powers helps the "Tan" republics safeguard their sovereignty and national interests while promoting regional peace and stability.

However, it is important to acknowledge and address any concerns regarding human rights and democracy promotion. Diplomats should engage in constructive dialogue with China, encouraging respect for human rights and democratic values while recognizing the importance of mutual respect and non-interference in internal affairs.

In conclusion, relations with China are a critical component of the foreign policy of the five "Tan" ex-Soviet republics. Diplomats must navigate the complexities of economic, energy, security, regional, cultural, and educational aspects of the relationship to ensure mutual benefits and promote peace, stability, and development.

Relations with the United States

In foreign policy, the five "Tan" ex-Soviet republics - Kazakhstan, Kyrgyzstan, Tajikistan, Turkmenistan, and Uzbekistan - have had a complex and evolving relationship with the United States. As diplomats representing these nations, it is crucial to understand the nuances of this relationship and navigate it effectively.

The United States plays a significant role in the foreign policy landscape of these countries. Historically, the U.S. has been a key partner in promoting economic development, security, and regional stability. The United States has provided financial assistance, technical expertise, and investment opportunities to support the growth of these nations' economies. It has also been instrumental in strengthening its security apparatus, particularly in combating terrorism and drug trafficking.

Furthermore, the United States has been an important ally for these countries in their efforts to build democratic institutions and protect human rights. Diplomats must engage with their American counterparts to foster dialogue and cooperation. This includes advocating for increased transparency, accountability, and respect for the rule of law.

However, it is important to acknowledge that the relationship between the five "Tan" ex-Soviet republics and the United States has its challenges. One key issue is the divergence in geopolitical interests. The United States has strategic concerns in the region, including energy security, counterterrorism, and the prevention of nuclear proliferation. These interests sometimes clash with the priorities of the "Tan" countries, leading to diplomatic tensions.

Border and territorial disputes are another aspect that can strain relations between these nations and the United States. Diplomats must navigate these sensitive issues carefully, promoting dialogue and peaceful resolutions while ensuring the interests of their respective countries are protected.

In recent years, efforts have been made to deepen the economic ties between the "Tan" countries and the United States. Trade and investment have become crucial components of their foreign policies, with diplomats working to attract American businesses and promote exports from their nations.

In summary, the relations between the five "Tan" ex-Soviet republics and the United States are multifaceted, encompassing economic, security, political, and cultural dimensions. Diplomats must skillfully navigate this relationship, balancing the interests of their countries and promoting cooperation on shared objectives while also addressing potential challenges and disputes.

Relations with the European Union

The five "Tan" ex-Soviet republics, namely Kazakhstan, Kyrgyzstan, Tajikistan, Turkmenistan, and Uzbekistan, have each developed unique relationships with the European Union (EU) over the years. This subchapter will provide an overview of the evolving diplomatic ties between these Central Asian nations and the EU, highlighting the key areas of cooperation and challenges faced.

The EU has been actively engaged in the region, aiming to promote stability, economic development, and democratic reforms. For the "Tan" republics, the EU represents an important partner in their foreign policy strategies, offering economic assistance, investment opportunities, and political dialogue.

Economically, the EU has played a significant role in supporting the development of these countries. The EU has provided financial aid, technical assistance, and trade preferences through various programs and initiatives to promote economic growth and reforms. This has helped the "Tan" republics to diversify their economies, enhance competitiveness, and improve their business environments.

Energy cooperation is another crucial aspect of the EU's relations with the "Tan" republics. Given the region's vast energy resources, particularly in Kazakhstan and Turkmenistan, the EU has pursued partnerships in the energy sector. This has involved projects such as the construction of pipelines and the promotion of renewable energy sources. These collaborations aim to enhance energy security in Europe and provide economic opportunities for the "Tan" republics.

Security cooperation has also been a priority for the EU in its relations with the "Tan" republics. Given their geographical location and shared borders with Afghanistan, these countries face various security challenges, including terrorism, drug trafficking, and organized crime. The EU has assisted in capacity building, border management, and counterterrorism efforts to enhance regional stability and security.

Regarding democratic reforms and human rights, the EU has played a crucial role in promoting good governance, the rule of law, and respect for human rights in the "Tan" republics. Through political dialogue, technical assistance, and financial support, the EU has encouraged these countries to enhance their democratic institutions, protect fundamental freedoms, and promote inclusivity and diversity.

However, challenges persist in the relations between the "Tan" republics and the EU. These include issues related to corruption, human rights violations, and the slow pace of democratic reforms. Furthermore, geopolitical considerations often influence the EU's engagement with these countries, including competing interests with other major powers.

In conclusion, the relations between the "Tan" ex-Soviet republics and the European Union have evolved over the years, encompassing various areas of cooperation. The EU's engagement has been instrumental in promoting economic development, energy security, regional stability, and democratic reforms. However, challenges remain, and continued efforts are needed to address these issues and further enhance the partnership between the "Tan" republics and the EU.

Relations with Other Major Powers

In the complex and ever-evolving landscape of international diplomacy, the five "Tan" ex-Soviet republics - Kazakhstan, Kyrgyzstan, Tajikistan, Turkmenistan, and Uzbekistan - are faced with the crucial task of managing their relations with other major powers. These relationships play a pivotal role in shaping the foreign policies of these nations and have far-reaching implications for their economic, energy, security, regional, cultural, and educational policies.

Diplomats representing the interests of the five "Tan" ex-Soviet republics must navigate a delicate balance between their historical ties to Russia and the growing influence of other major powers. While Russia remains a significant partner, the increasing engagement of China, the United States, and the European Union presents unique opportunities and challenges for these nations.

China's Belt and Road Initiative has become a major focal point in the region. The five "Tan" republics have sought to leverage their strategic location to benefit from China's massive infrastructure investments. They have actively pursued partnerships with China to enhance their economic development, trade, and connectivity. However, diplomats must carefully manage these relationships to ensure they do not compromise their national interests or fall into a debt trap.

The United States and the European Union also play important roles in shaping the foreign policies of the five "Tan" ex-Soviet republics. These powers offer valuable support in democracy promotion, human rights, and economic cooperation. Diplomats must engage with these partners to foster mutually beneficial relationships that contribute to the stability and development of their nations.

Furthermore, regional cooperation and integration are vital for the five "Tan" ex-Soviet republics. Diplomats must actively engage with organizations such as the Eurasian Economic Union, the Shanghai Cooperation Organization, and the Commonwealth of Independent States to promote regional stability, resolve border and territorial disputes, and enhance trade and investment opportunities.

However, managing relations with major powers also poses challenges. The five "Tan" republics must navigate these powers' competing interests and rivalries without compromising their sovereignty or national security. Diplomats must skillfully negotiate and mediate to ensure that these relationships contribute to the overall well-being of their nations.

In conclusion, the five "Tan" ex-Soviet republics face a complex web of diplomatic relations with major powers. Diplomats are crucial in managing these relationships to advance their nation's economic, energy, security, regional, cultural, and educational interests. By skillfully navigating these dynamics, they can establish mutually beneficial partnerships that contribute to the prosperity and stability of the five "Tan" republics.

Chapter 11: Human Rights and Democracy Promotion

Human Rights Challenges in Kazakhstan

Like other ex-Soviet republics, Kazakhstan faces significant human rights challenges that pose complex dilemmas for diplomats engaged in foreign policy in the region. While Kazakhstan has made strides in economic development and regional cooperation, promoting and protecting human rights remain areas of concern.

One of the key challenges in Kazakhstan is restricting freedom of expression and press freedom. The government has been criticized for suppressing dissenting voices and independent media outlets. Journalists and activists face harassment, intimidation, and even imprisonment for expressing their views or investigating sensitive issues. Diplomats must navigate these challenges delicately, as advocating for press freedom and freedom of expression can strain diplomatic relations.

Another issue of concern is the lack of political pluralism and the limited space for opposition parties and civil society organizations to operate. The ruling party dominates the political landscape, and opposition figures often face obstacles such as arbitrary arrests and restrictions on their activities. Diplomats must engage with the government to promote a more inclusive political environment that allows for genuine political competition and the participation of diverse voices.

Furthermore, Kazakhstan struggles with protecting minority rights, particularly those of ethnic and religious minorities. Discrimination and marginalization persist, and there have been reports of restrictions on religious practices and the suppression of cultural identity.

Diplomats must address these challenges by advocating for the full inclusion and equal treatment of all individuals, regardless of ethnicity or religion.

Additionally, Kazakhstan's justice system has raised concerns regarding fair trials and due process. Reports of corruption, political interference, and torture during interrogations have raised questions about the credibility and effectiveness of the judiciary. Diplomats must strengthen the rule of law and ensure that all individuals have access to a fair and impartial justice system.

In conclusion, human rights challenges in Kazakhstan present complex obstacles for diplomats engaged in foreign policy in the region. Diplomats must address issues such as freedom of expression, political pluralism, minority rights, and the independence of the judiciary. By advocating for human rights and democracy, diplomats can contribute to developing a more inclusive and just society in Kazakhstan.

Human Rights Challenges in Kyrgyzstan

Like its neighboring ex-Soviet republics, Kyrgyzstan faces several human rights challenges that must be addressed in its foreign policy. This subchapter will delve into the specific human rights issues within Kyrgyzstan and the strategies diplomats can employ to promote human rights and democracy in the country.

One of Kyrgyzstan's primary human rights challenges is the lack of freedom of expression and media freedom. Journalists and activists face harassment, intimidation, and violence when they attempt to report on sensitive issues or criticize the government. Diplomats can play a crucial role in advocating for the protection of journalists and press freedom through diplomatic channels and public statements.

Another concern is the discrimination and violence against minority groups, particularly the Uzbek population. The interethnic violence erupted in 2010 between Kyrgyz and Uzbeks, resulting in numerous casualties and the displacement of thousands of people. Diplomats can work with the Kyrgyz government to ensure that minority rights are protected and promote reconciliation between different ethnic groups.

The treatment of women and gender-based violence is another critical human rights challenge in Kyrgyzstan. Domestic violence, early and forced marriages, and bride kidnappings are prevalent in the country. Diplomats can collaborate with local women's rights organizations to address these issues and push for legal reforms that protect women's rights.

Furthermore, the lack of an independent judiciary and corruption within the legal system undermines the rule of law in Kyrgyzstan. Diplomats can advocate for judicial reforms and support initiatives that promote transparency and accountability within the judiciary.

Lastly, the rights of the LGBTQ+ community face significant challenges in Kyrgyzstan. Homophobia and discrimination against the LGBTQ+ community are widespread, and the government has passed laws restricting their rights and freedoms. Diplomats can engage with local LGBTQ+ organizations and raise these concerns with the Kyrgyz government to encourage dialogue and progress on LGBTQ+ rights.

In conclusion, Kyrgyzstan faces several human rights challenges requiring diplomats' attention and action. By advocating for freedom of expression, minority rights, women's rights, judicial reforms, and LGBTQ+ rights, diplomats can contribute to promoting human rights and democracy in Kyrgyzstan. Diplomats must prioritize these issues in their foreign policy engagements and work collaboratively with the Kyrgyz government and civil society to address these challenges effectively.

Human Rights Challenges in Tajikistan

Tajikistan, one of the five "Tan" ex-Soviet republics, presents unique challenges regarding human rights and democracy promotion. As diplomats navigating the foreign policy landscape of these countries, it is essential to understand and address the human rights issues faced by Tajikistan.

One of the major human rights challenges in Tajikistan is restricting freedom of expression and the press. The government maintains tight control over the media, limiting critical voices and independent journalism. Journalists are often subjected to harassment, intimidation, and even violence, hindering the free flow of information and stifling public discourse.

Another pressing issue is the lack of political pluralism and the limited space for opposition parties. The ruling party dominates the political scene, making it difficult for alternative voices to be heard. This lack of political competition undermines democratic processes and the ability of citizens to participate in decision-making.

Tajikistan also faces challenges in the area of religious freedom. The government has imposed restrictive measures on religious practices, particularly targeting Islamic groups. This has led to the marginalization of certain religious communities and the violation of their fundamental rights.

Furthermore, Tajikistan struggles with issues related to torture and ill-treatment in detention facilities. Reports of abuse, including beatings and electric shocks, have emerged, highlighting the need for improved prison conditions and the protection of detainees' rights.

Addressing these human rights challenges requires a comprehensive approach. Diplomats can be crucial in advocating for reforms and engaging in dialogue with the Tajik government. This includes urging the authorities to respect freedom of expression and the press, encouraging political pluralism, and promoting religious tolerance.

Additionally, diplomatic efforts can focus on strengthening the rule of law and ensuring accountability for human rights violations. This may involve supporting initiatives to improve prison conditions, enhance the independence of the judiciary, and establish effective mechanisms for investigating and prosecuting cases of torture and ill-treatment.

Furthermore, diplomats can collaborate with international organizations and civil society groups to monitor human rights conditions in Tajikistan. By raising awareness and providing support to local human rights defenders, diplomats can contribute to promoting and protecting human rights in the country.

In conclusion, Tajikistan faces significant human rights challenges, including restrictions on freedom of expression, limited political pluralism, religious freedom violations, and issues related to torture and ill-treatment. Diplomats must actively engage with the Tajik government, advocate for reforms, and support initiatives that promote human rights and democracy in the country.

Human Rights Challenges in Turkmenistan

In human rights, Turkmenistan has faced significant challenges over the years. As diplomats navigating the foreign policy landscape of the five "Tan" ex-Soviet republics, it is crucial to understand the human rights situation in Turkmenistan to engage with the country and promote positive change effectively.

Turkmenistan is known for its authoritarian regime, where political dissent is heavily suppressed and basic freedoms are limited. Freedom of expression, assembly, and association are severely restricted, with independent media outlets and civil society organizations facing constant harassment and intimidation. The government exercises tight control over all aspects of society, including the judiciary and educational institutions, limiting the space for dissent and critical thinking.

One of Turkmenistan's most pressing human rights concerns is the treatment of political prisoners. Many individuals who have dared to criticize the government or advocate for human rights have been subjected to arbitrary detention, torture, and unfair trials. Their families often face harassment and intimidation, creating a climate of fear that further stifles dissent.

Another significant challenge is the lack of transparency and accountability in Turkmenistan. The government operates with little oversight, and corruption is pervasive. This not only hampers the country's economic development but also undermines human rights, as resources allocated to improving living conditions for the population are misappropriated.

Furthermore, Turkmenistan has a poor record of freedom of religion and belief. The state heavily regulates religious practices and restricts the activities of religious groups, particularly those deemed "non-traditional." This has led to discrimination and persecution against religious minorities, limiting their ability to practice their faith freely.

As diplomats, addressing these human rights challenges in Turkmenistan is crucial through diplomatic engagement and dialogue. By raising these issues with the Turkmen government, encouraging respect for human rights, and offering support and assistance to civil society organizations, we can contribute to positive change in the country.

Moreover, working with international partners and organizations is important to pressure the Turkmen government to improve its human rights record. Through multilateral platforms, we can coordinate efforts to advocate for releasing political prisoners, improve freedom of expression and association, and establish transparent and accountable governance structures.

In conclusion, Turkmenistan faces significant human rights challenges, including restrictions on political freedoms, lack of transparency and accountability, and limitations on freedom of religion and belief. As diplomats, we are responsible for engaging with the Turkmen government and international partners to address these challenges, promote human rights, and work towards a more inclusive and democratic society in Turkmenistan.

Human Rights Challenges in Uzbekistan

Uzbekistan, one of the five "Tan" ex-Soviet republics, faces significant challenges in human rights. As diplomats navigating the foreign policy landscape of these countries, it is crucial to address the human rights situation in Uzbekistan and advocate for positive change.

Uzbekistan has been criticized for its limited political freedoms, restricted media, and lack of an independent judiciary. The country's government has been accused of suppressing opposition voices, stifling freedom of speech, and curtailing civil liberties. Human rights organizations have documented cases of torture, arbitrary detentions, and forced labour in Uzbekistan.

One of the key challenges in promoting human rights in Uzbekistan is the government's lack of transparency and accountability. The country's authoritarian regime has maintained a tight grip on power, making it difficult for civil society organizations and international observers to monitor and address human rights abuses effectively.

Furthermore, the human rights situation is intertwined with other issues, such as corruption and economic development. Addressing human rights challenges requires a holistic approach considering the social, political, and economic factors. Diplomats must engage with Uzbekistan's government and civil society to encourage reforms and ensure that human rights are prioritized in the country's development agenda.

International alliances and partnerships are crucial in promoting human rights in Uzbekistan. Diplomats must leverage their relationships with other nations and international organizations to pressure the Uzbek government to improve its human rights record. Engaging in dialogues and negotiations can lead to meaningful reforms and encourage Uzbekistan to meet its international obligations.

Diplomatic efforts should also focus on supporting and strengthening civil society organizations in Uzbekistan. These groups play a vital role in advocating for human rights and providing a voice for marginalized communities. Diplomats can provide financial assistance, capacity building, and other forms of support to empower these organizations and amplify their impact.

In conclusion, the human rights challenges in Uzbekistan are significant and require sustained diplomatic efforts. As diplomats navigating the foreign policy landscape of the five "Tan" ex-Soviet republics, it is essential to recognize and address these challenges. By engaging with the Uzbek government, supporting civil society, and leveraging international partnerships, diplomats can contribute to promoting human rights and democracy in Uzbekistan.

Conclusion: Navigating the Foreign Policy Landscape: A Diplomat's Guide to the Five "Tan" Ex-Soviet Republics

In conclusion, understanding the foreign policy landscape of the five "Tan" ex-Soviet republics - Kazakhstan, Kyrgyzstan, Tajikistan, Turkmenistan, and Uzbekistan - is crucial for diplomats navigating the complex geopolitical dynamics of Central Asia. This guide has provided valuable insights into the various aspects of their foreign policies, shedding light on the economic, energy, security, regional, cultural, educational, trade, investment, international alliance, border and territorial dispute, diplomatic relations, and human rights and democracy promotion dimensions.

The economic foreign policy of these republics has been characterized by a shift towards diversification and attracting foreign investment. Diplomats must be aware of each country's unique economic opportunities and challenges, as well as the potential for regional cooperation and integration.

Energy plays a pivotal role in the foreign policy of the "Tan" republics, with rich oil, gas, and minerals reserves. Understanding the energy dynamics and their implications for domestic and international relations is essential for diplomats seeking to engage with these countries effectively.

Security is a key concern in the region, given its proximity to conflict zones and the threat of terrorism. Diplomats must be well-versed in each country's security policies and challenges, including border and territorial disputes, to foster stability and peace.

Regional foreign policy is crucial for the "Tan" republics as they seek to balance their relationships with neighboring countries and regional organizations. Diplomats must navigate the intricacies of regional dynamics, including multilateral agreements and cooperation frameworks.

Cultural and educational foreign policy has emerged as a tool for soft power projection as these republics seek to promote their rich cultural heritage and educational opportunities. Diplomats should engage in cultural exchanges and educational collaborations to deepen people-to-people ties.

Trade and investment foreign policy is vital for these republics' economic growth and development. Diplomats must identify potential trade partners and investment opportunities, facilitating business interactions and promoting economic cooperation.

International alliances and partnerships play a significant role in shaping the foreign policy of the "Tan" republics. Diplomats must foster relationships with major powers and international organizations to leverage support for their national interests.

Addressing border and territorial disputes is crucial for regional stability. Diplomats must engage in dialogue and mediation efforts to resolve these longstanding issues peacefully.

Diplomatic relations with major powers are instrumental in shaping the foreign policy of the "Tan" republics. Diplomats should cultivate strong ties with influential nations to advance their national interests and ensure regional stability.

Finally, promoting human rights and democracy is a crucial aspect of foreign policy for the "Tan" republics. Diplomats should engage in dialogue and cooperation to encourage progress in these areas while respecting each country's sovereignty and cultural sensitivities.

In conclusion, diplomats must comprehensively understand the foreign policy landscape of the five "Tan" ex-Soviet republics to effectively navigate Central Asia's complex dynamics. By considering the economic, energy, security, regional, cultural, educational, trade, investment, international alliance, border and territorial dispute, diplomatic relations, and human rights and democracy promotion dimensions, diplomats can foster peace, stability, and prosperity in the region.